# Super
# Energy
# Detox

# Super Energy Detox

## 21-Day Plan

with 60 Allergy-Free Recipes

**Antoinette Savill
and Dawn Hamilton**

Thorsons

Thorsons
An Imprint of HarperCollins*Publishers*
77–85 Fulham Palace Road,
Hammersmith, London W6 8JB

The Thorsons website address is:
www.thorsons.com

and *Thorsons* are trademarks of
HarperCollins*Publishers* Ltd

First published by Thorsons 2002

10 9 8 7 6 5 4 3 2 1

Text © Dawn Hamilton 2002
Recipes © Antoinette Savill 2002

Antoinette Savill and Dawn Hamilton assert the moral
right to be identified as the authors of this work

A catalogue record of this book is available
from the British Library

ISBN 0 00 713399 5

Printed and bound in Great Britain by
Creative Print and Design (Wales), Ebbw Vale

# Contents

## chapter 1

# The Super Energy Detox

Life deserves to be lived to the full. The world we live in is a wonderful place. Even if we lived to be 500 it's doubtful we could experience all the gifts it offers, but if we are going to enjoy life to the full we need to have a healthy body. This doesn't just mean a body that hasn't got a disease: it means a vibrant, energized and balanced body that can fully engage in the activities we choose.

The food you eat significantly impacts on the way you feel, the amount of energy you have, how you look and your overall health. Certain types of foods decrease your energy levels and dull the mind; these same foods can be difficult for your body to assimilate so they put a strain on parts of its elimination system, such as the digestive tract. As this system becomes overburdened, you may find that you start to succumb to minor complaints like digestive problems, frequent headaches, poor skin and mild depression. This perpetuating cycle, along with other factors such as stress, overwork and difficult relationships, can result in your living life in monochrome rather than full technicolour.

## Why detox?

If you're fed up with wearing grey and would like to experience more of the magic and sparkle of life, you need to give your body a chance to restore and revitalize itself. One of the easiest and most effective ways of doing this is to follow a safe and gentle detox programme. Detoxing is not a new concept – people in all cultures throughout civilization have practiced it. Ancient yogis developed highly sophisticated methods of cleansing thousands of years ago, and natural healing centres in Europe have been using detox programmes to treat a variety of conditions for the past 200 years. While we now understand the scientific principles behind the detox process, the basic underlying concepts remain the same, and the fact that such concepts have survived over the years attests to the numerous benefits – physical, emotional, mental and spiritual – that occur when you follow such a programme.

The Super Energy Detox combines these long-held principles with current insights from modern-day natural healing. It is a very gentle, yet highly effective, programme that can be followed at the same time as your normal day-to-day activities. I have enjoyed the benefits first hand and I hope you will too.

## Food intolerance and detoxing

Food intolerance is a condition that is associated with many chronic health problems, such as lack of energy, irritable bowel, bloating, fluid retention, menstrual tension, depression and skin complaints. Because of the diverse nature of these symptoms, a food intolerance problem can go undiagnosed for years and it's easy to see how this can have a substantial impact on your quality of life. The good news is that food intolerance doesn't need to be a life-long sentence for the vast majority of sufferers. Provided the correct steps are taken, it's possible to stop reacting to trigger foods and so to avoid debilitating symptoms.

A food intolerance condition is closely connected to the health and functioning of the body's elimination system, therefore, along with avoiding culprit foods, detoxing is a great first step towards dealing with the condition. This is because the detox process involves working with the major organs and channels of the elimination system: when the elimination system is functioning well, there is significantly less chance of negative food reactions occurring.

## An overview of the programme

The Super Energy Detox lasts for three weeks, and consists of four distinct elements.

### 1 Foods and juices

Recommended foods are those that support the body's elimination system and your overall health, and the choice of these foods is based on certain key underlying principles. They include foods that have an alkalizing effect on the body and foods that are high in nutrients and enzymes. These nourish the body and help create the right conditions for it to cleanse itself. Juicing is an integral component of this programme and you will be introduced to some special detox juice formulas.

### 2 Cleansing substances

These are nutritional and herbal formulations that help the body's elimination system to remove old and unnecessary waste matter. They are all based on only natural ingredients and the action they have on the body is very gentle.

### 3 Energy exercises

This is a series of different exercises that boost and invigorate your body's energy system. Spending just a few minutes each day practising them can give you many benefits, including helping you to manage stress more effectively. They also support the body while it's going through the cleansing process.

### 4 Lifestyle projects

These are fun and interesting activities that help increase the effectiveness of the detox programme. There are also lots of useful tips and suggestions for improving your home environment so your exposure to toxins and pollutants is reduced. You are free to choose those that appeal to you most.

The detox programme is divided into weeks, with clear instructions on what you need to do each week. You will also have the opportunity to personalize the programme according to your own particular needs (page 54).

## Summer and winter detox

The Super Energy Detox consists of two eating plans, one each for summer and winter. Changing your diet along with the seasons means you will be working in harmony with the body's natural rhythms. Summer is the best time to enjoy a detox diet of lots of raw foods such as salads and fruits because the body can assimilate these foods easily at this time of year. However, a diet containing a lot of raw foods is not beneficial during the winter because it can put a strain on your elimination system, especially the digestive tract. Winter is best suited to a detox diet of warming foods such as roasted vegetables and rich, nourishing soups. Antoinette has provided healthy and tasty recipes for both of these seasons.

## The maintenance programme

This aspect of the Super Energy Detox is designed specifically for people who have a food intolerance condition. It contains healthy eating guidelines to follow after completing the detox, and it also outlines certain nutritional strategies that can help strengthen the underlying body systems (such as the digestive tract) often involved in a food intolerance problem. I recommend that the maintenance programme is followed for about two to four months, and there are plenty of recipes to try during this period.

## When to start

You can start this programme at any time. If the weather is warm and sunny, follow the summer eating plan. In winter, a good time to start is just after Christmas and New Year – it's an excellent way of recovering from the excesses of this period and it also fits well with the symbolism of a new and fresh start to the year.

## How to use this book

The first seven chapters introduce the key concepts you will be working with on the programme. Chapter Two looks at the meaning of health and explains how to understand the cause of minor symptoms. Chapter Three discusses how detoxing can improve your health and help you reconnect to your intrinsic body wisdom. Chapter Four is devoted to the topic of food intolerance: it addresses the link between intolerance and the elimination system and shows how people who might have this condition can benefit from the detox programme.

The dietary and lifestyle strategies you will be following during the programme are intended to support the functioning of the elimination system. In order for you to have a clear understanding of why you are following these recommendations, Chapters Five to Seven explore how this system functions.

You can read these chapters sequentially or dip into the parts that interest you most. If you choose to do the latter, please make sure you complete the questionnaires in Chapters Three and Four as these are useful indicators of certain aspects of your current health and well-being.

Chapter Eight onwards concentrates on putting the programme into practice.

## Personalizing your programme

Before you start you are given the opportunity to personalize the programme according to your individual needs, and for this you need to do a series of questionnaires in Chapter Nine. This should be more beneficial than a 'one size fits all' approach, and everything you need to do is clearly specified and broken down into easy-to-follow steps.

## Using the questionnaires

I have designed these to help you identify various health and nutritional conditions – including food intolerance, yeast sensitivity and how well the individual channels of your elimination system are functioning.

By their very nature, questionnaires are always limited, so answering a series of questions can't confirm conclusively that you have a food intolerance problem, but it can indicate that you *might* have an intolerance. If this is the case, it would then be useful for you to either consult a nutritionist who can arrange proper biochemical tests, or follow an elimination trial (page 245). At the same time you should also consult your doctor to rule out the existence of other factors that might be the cause of your symptoms.

So bear in mind that the questionnaires are only for guidance to help you personalize the programme: they are not a means of self-diagnosis. A particular symptom may be associated with a particular nutritional condition, but it may not, so make sure you get proper advice from a doctor or another suitably qualified health-care professional.

## What you will need

You will get excellent results on the programme just by following the eating guidelines and practising the energy exercises, but you will get even better results by including other recommendations such as juicing, skin brushing and nutritional supplementation. For these you need to get certain items of equipment such as a juice extractor (you can keep using the extractor after the programme so it won't end up gathering dust). If you're not keen on taking nutritional or herbal supplements, simply omit this part of the programme. The specific cleansing substances you will need are discussed in Chapter Ten. Strategies for integrating this programme into your daily routine are in Chapter Eleven.

## Who shouldn't follow the programme?

Do not follow the Super Energy Detox if you are:

- pregnant, trying to become pregnant, or breastfeeding.
- currently suffering with a serious illness, recovering from a serious illness, or using any form of prescribed or non-prescribed medication.

- seriously underweight.
- suffering with an eating disorder.
- have any type of psychological complaint.

If you are in any doubt, seek proper medical advice.

## A way of life

A regular gentle detox once or twice a year is one of the best things you can do to look after your body, but what's even more important is looking after yourself 365 days of the year. A short-term cleanse isn't going to achieve all that much if your principal diet for the rest of the year consists of processed foods and takeaways.

This programme works best when it forms part of an overall healthy lifestyle, and one of the effects that people often experience after a detox is to naturally move towards a healthier diet in the long term – because high-sugar, high-fat and heavily processed foods no longer hold the same appeal. The maintenance programme provides you with strategies to build on the benefits you have experienced from the detox, while the energy exercises are excellent when included in your normal routine as they help balance and improve your energy levels. Practising them on an on-going basis can also help make you more resilient to stress.

## chapter 2

# The Health Spectrum

## What is health?

If you ask most people whether they are healthy they will generally say yes. The usual way of defining health is in terms of the absence of disease – we think that if we're not under the care of a doctor or taking prescribed medication then we must be healthy. Of course, in one sense this is absolutely correct, but to look at health purely in such restrictive terms as the absence of illness is doing ourselves an injustice and cheating us out of the full potential of what health can really be.

Health should be viewed as a spectrum, not as something you either have or haven't got. At the lower end of the spectrum there is illness and disease, at the top there is total health. Most of us actually live somewhere in the middle – we might not have an identifiable disease, but we're not totally healthy either. When we're living around the middle of the health spectrum, we think it's okay to tolerate all sorts of symptoms and complaints and we probably think they're just a normal part of living. Headaches, poor skin, back pain, stiff muscles, indigestion, constipation, lack of energy, joint pains, arthritis, period pains, pre-menstrual tension and frequent colds are generally considered to be part and parcel of life.

The next time you go shopping, take a look at the range of over-the-counter medications on offer – there's something for just about every conceivable type of ache or pain. There are tablets to make you go to the loo and tablets to stop you going; capsules to stop your stomach producing too much acid; potions to stop your skin having spots; pills to pep you up and pills to calm you down. The worldwide pharmaceutical market is big business, accounting for over $300 billion of sales a year. Of course, prescribed medication has its place – it saves lives – but do we really need this many over-the-counter drugs? Do they actually help us or are they just a short-term solution that suppresses symptoms without providing a proper cure?

Scientists believe the human life span is actually in the region of 120 rather than the current 80 years, yet if you were to ask most people if they'd like to live to 120 they'd usually respond with a definite no. When we're existing in the middle of the health spectrum, we regard ageing as a totally negative process, we see the later years of life as just a dire existence with a feeble body and mind, and it's no wonder that the thought of living to 120 fills us with horror. Thankfully there are plenty of healthy, lively octogenarians and nonagenarians to act as positive role models so we know we don't have to be doomed to this fate.

## Moving towards full health

Full health means that your physical body is functioning at its peak. You wake up in the morning bright-eyed and ready to seize the day, and you rarely resort to pills and potions to relieve the sorts of discomfort described above. Your mind is clear and sharp and you feel great, you have a good relationship with your body, you enjoy the full range of sensations it offers. You laugh a lot and are frequently happy.

Defining health in these terms isn't the full picture, because you are much more than just a physical body – you function as an integrated being with emotional, mental and spiritual dimensions as well. How balanced you are on these other levels impacts on both your physical health and your overall well-being. Any 'dis-ease' you experience on an emotional, mental or spiritual level is bound to impact on the health of the physical body and vice versa.

To say that you are completely healthy implies that all levels of your being are working well and are in a dynamic balance. It means that your emotional life is rich and flowing. This suggests that you are aware of your feelings and deal with them in a healthy way, and it also means that your mental faculties are functioning well and that you use them to create a purpose and meaning to your life. It also means that you feel comfortable with who you are and those around you.

Of course, there are no magic potions that can inoculate us against physical disease, nor are there any strategies that guarantee we will only ever feel positive emotions and never feel emotional pain – illness and emotional suffering are part of the human condition. To my knowledge, no one lives a perfect life and enjoys perfect health – in the full definition – all of the time. Change is the one constant that we all experience. In essence, the health spectrum is a road that we continually travel along, rather than any particular destination that we arrive at.

Despite recent advances in medicine, modern life generally does a pretty poor job of promoting full health. A diet consisting of refined and processed foods doesn't help the body perform at its best, and yet to move further along the health spectrum towards better health and greater vitality isn't that difficult. A healthy diet, managing emotions in a healthy fashion and creating a life that truly reflects who you really are on a deeper level can shift you a long way along the spectrum, and detoxing is a great way of starting the process. What will also help on this journey is the ability to understand and respond effectively to the messages that are constantly coming from your body.

## The body's messages

I've already mentioned that minor physical symptoms are generally assumed to be part and parcel of life. We tolerate them rather than looking more closely and considering what they mean. The body is constantly communicating with us – it lets us know when it's hungry and when it needs sleep. Without these signals, how would we know it's time to eat or to rest? It also tells us when it's too hot or cold so we can take action to feel comfortable again. We're all aware of these major signals, but there are many other, more subtle, messages that we may fail to notice or understand.

Any form of discomfort is simply the body's way of letting us know that something isn't right. Physical discomfort may not be pleasant, but it's very useful – it's the body's way of communicating its needs.

Headache, a common symptom of physical discomfort, is a useful example to illustrate this point. It can have multiple causes, ranging from eye strain and a build-up of emotional stress to cranial constriction or even a more serious underlying illness. Yet from a nutritional point of view, two of the most common causes of headaches are skipping meals (which results in low blood sugar) and insufficient fluid intake. The headache may be the body's way of saying 'can I have some food and water?' or 'you need to have your glasses checked', but quite often we simply miss the message and we resort to taking a painkiller instead. Whatever caused the situation in the first place is still there; all we've achieved is a dulling of the signal.

The body's messages extend far further than simply telling us about the physical aspect of our lives. How do we actually know we are feeling happy, loving, sad, angry or depressed? It's only possible to experience these emotions from the sensations we receive from our bodies. For example, anger usually manifests itself as a tightening in the stomach and feeling hot, whereas falling in love often gives us warm, fuzzy feelings in the middle of our chest.

Because we live in a culture that values the mind above the body, this is a concept that can be quite difficult to grasp. Try this short experiment to make the concept more real for you. How are you feeling right now? Just answer with the first thing that comes to mind. Now try to look a little closer by focusing on how your body is feeling at this moment. Close your eyes for a few seconds and take your attention into your body. What physical and emotional sensations can you observe? It's probable that you noticed a great deal more about how you were feeling when you took a few seconds to focus on your body.

We tend to live such busy lives that our attention is mainly focused on the world outside – it's relatively rare to be still, focus inwardly and listen to what our bodies and emotions are trying to tell us. Understanding the body's communication system is akin to learning a new foreign language – it takes time and practice to know how to decode these signals into useful information. Furthermore, everyone's body communication system is different, so there is a unique language to be learned by each of us.

When we are able to interpret our body's unique signals, life can become much easier. For example, your body's inner wisdom intrinsically recognizes the foods that support your health. The craving for strange food combinations that pregnant women often experience is an example of this in action – somehow the body knows that a banana sandwich at 3am is just what the body and the growing baby needs. When you pay attention to your body's emotional signals, you are better placed to take action to change your life for the better.

One way of furthering your understanding of the messages your body sends you is to learn how your body functions. In Chapters Five, Six and Seven I describe how the individual elements of the elimination system function and how they can provide you with a road map to help you interpret what the signs and signals mean. For example, when you understand how the digestive system works you will have a clearer idea of why certain common digestive complaints occur, and this will help you deal with the underlying cause of a symptom in a natural way rather than covering it up with an over-the-counter medication.

While dietary factors are obviously important, symptoms such as headaches, indigestion and muscular aches and pains often sneak up on us as a result of a build-up of emotional stress during the day. Two excellent exercises to use whenever you notice you are getting off balance in this way are belly breathing (page 92) and the grounding sequence described on page 108. Spending just a couple of minutes doing either of these exercises can break the stress cycle and get you centred again. This will help put you back in touch with your body so you can determine what these messages are telling you about your eating habits, emotions and general lifestyle.

## Reconnecting to this system: the value of detoxing

One of the main, but often overlooked, benefits of detoxing is that it can put you back in touch with this sophisticated communication system, and the effect of being able to listen to your body's messages better can have far-reaching benefits for both your health and your life in general. Reconnecting with your body's innate wisdom is a great way of progressing further up the health spectrum – signals of discomfort no longer need to be ignored and suppressed. Instead, you will be able to recognize what these messages mean and you can then take steps to change your diet and lifestyle for the better so the symptoms no longer occur.

The reason detoxing has this effect is because of the strong link between diet and the effectiveness of the body's ability to communicate to us. A diet high in fatty, sugary and processed foods, stimulants and alcohol dulls this communication network between our minds and our bodies. This is where the phrase 'drowning our sorrows' comes from – drinking alcohol can stop you feeling your emotions in the same way that a painkiller stops you feeling the pain of a headache. The problem is that too much alcohol doesn't just drown your sorrows, it drowns your joys as well, because it affects your ability to feel *all* emotions – not merely the painful ones you are trying to avoid. This doesn't mean that alcohol should be avoided completely – there's nothing wrong with moderate amounts – it's the underlying reasons for drinking that are important.

A diet of refined and processed foods can have a dulling effect on the body's communication network because it puts a lot of strain on the elimination system (especially the digestive system and the liver). Food intolerance also reduces your vitality and your body's ability to communicate effectively with you because of the extra burden it places on the elimination system. Unfortunately, these effects tend to sneak up on you gradually until you reach the point where you accept symptoms such as frequent tiredness, bloating and headaches as the norm.

Conversely, a diet of alkalizing and nutrient-rich foods, such as those you'll be eating on the detox, makes this communication system much more vibrant. You will feel more energized and mentally clear, your body will feel more alive and aware of how you are feeling both emotionally and physically on a day-to-day basis. After following the programme you will probably notice you are much more aware how certain foods affect your mood, energy levels and physical health. This has nothing to do with knowing more about nutrition, it's an awareness coming from the messages your body gives you.

At this level, you can choose which foods to eat according to these messages, and this can pay big dividends for your health in the long term. It's an important point, because there's no single eating plan that is perfect for everybody – each one of us has unique nutritional needs – and our individual nutritional requirements can change over time. For example, your body is likely to require different types of foods when you're working really hard from those it needs when you're on holiday. It's much better to follow your body's messages regarding diet than to follow an eating plan given to you by somebody else. But to get to the point where you are able to receive clear messages from your body you need to create the right internal environment where this system can operate properly.

## chapter 3

# The Process of Detoxing

In the previous chapter, health wasn't defined as a static state but as a spectrum. Undertaking a gentle detox programme like the one here is one of the best ways of moving further along this health spectrum. Detoxing can produce numerous benefits to health – here is a list of some of them:

- A significant increase in energy levels.
- Thinking processes become clearer and sharper.
- Mood improves and life's problems seem less significant.
- Skin takes on a radiant glow and eyes become bright and clear.
- Hair becomes more shiny.
- Cellulite diminishes.
- Excess bloating and fluid retention can disappear.
- Minor health complaints can clear up.
- Food cravings decline.
- Heightened awareness of emotions and feelings.
- Heightened awareness of how your diet and lifestyle affects your well-being.
- Life takes on more sparkle and you feel more alive and vibrant.

Many of these benefits start to emerge within a short period of time, often within 10 days or so of starting the programme. Then, provided a healthy diet is followed, the benefits of the detox will stay with you long after the programme has ended. You should find that you are living much nearer the top end of the health spectrum, and that you no longer need to tolerate minor complaints as an accepted part of life.

## The amazing body

Why is it that detoxing can produce all these benefits? While we're busy with our jobs, having fun with friends, making love or just sitting watching a beautiful sunset, our bodies are continuously working hard to keep us in good health. We're exposed to a deluge of bacteria and viruses on a daily basis, but most of the time the body's defence system stops these invaders in their tracks and ensures we don't get ill.

The dust in our houses consists primarily of dead skin cells. Our bodies dispose of these cells – and worn-out or damaged cells from all over our bodies – and replaces them with new ones. In fact, regular cellular repair means that every seven years or so you have a completely brand new body (including new bones). Your own body does all of this – and a great deal more – 24 hours a day, 365 days a year.

The body has a highly sophisticated self-cleaning system that is constantly working to maintain a safe internal environment. Without the activities of the elimination system, vital bodily functions could not perform as normal. This system, which consists of the digestive tract, liver, lymph, lungs, kidneys and skin, also has a direct influence on how we feel. When it is working well we are likely to enjoy a high level of health and vitality, but when it is not functioning as well as it could we probably feel below par.

We often don't notice how the dust and grime build up in our homes because it happens over a period of time, but we definitely notice the difference after we've spent some time spring-cleaning. In a similar way, we might not be aware of the gradual decline in our levels of energy and vitality. Going on a detox has the same effect as a good spring-clean, and it's only afterwards that we realize how under the weather we were before.

## Toxins and the body

Toxins are not new: there has always been a certain level of toxic sub-stances in the environment. These include organic contaminants natu-rally found in the soil and the toxic compounds found in some foods and herbs. In fact, the body also produces a large amount of toxic by-products each and every day. Normal activities such as breathing, moving about, fighting off infections and assimilating the nutrients we get from food produce a whole range of different molecular substances that have a toxic effect on the system. Many of these molecular reactions involve oxygen and, while we need oxygen to stay alive, it also has damaging effects. If you cut an apple in half and leave it exposed to the air the flesh will turn brown within a few minutes – this is damage caused by oxygen. It acts in a similar fashion within the body when it is involved in functions such as cellular metabolism.

The body is well equipped to deal with toxic substances and the potentially damaging effect of oxygen reactions. If the elimination system is functioning well and the supply of antioxidant nutrients and enzymes is adequate, it will safely de-activate the potentially harmful by-products of respiration, metabolism and immune function. The same is true for a moderate level of environmental toxins, but if these molecules are not properly de-activated and eliminated they can cause damage to DNA and increase the risk of disease.

If the exposure to external toxins is in balance with the body's ability to de-activate these compounds, there is likely to be minimal damage to your health. However, if your exposure to toxins is increased and/or the body's ability to deal with these substances is reduced, then you are potentially creating conditions for numerous types of health problems to occur. Everybody is aware of the level of pollutants in our food, water and environment; a less well-known source of pollution comes from hydrogenated fats (also called trans-fats) which are a very recent addition to our diet. They are found in vegetable spreads and they're used in a large percentage of processed foods.

Dietary fats, especially polyunsaturates such as sunflower and saf-flower oil, are particularly vulnerable to molecular damage when exposed to either heat or oxygen. Uncovered oils and butter will quickly turn rancid due to the chemical interaction that occurs with oxygen.

The manufacturing process that converts an oil (such as sunflower) into a hydrogenated fat (such as sunflower spread) involves exposing the oil to high temperatures, and this causes extensive damage to the oil at a molecular level. Eating foods that contain hydrogenated fats is another source of stress to both the body and the elimination system; they are very bad for the body and should be avoided.

Exposure to environmental and dietary pollutants is continually on the increase while our consumption of antioxidant nutrients and enzymes is in decline. For example, our consumption of selenium (an important antioxidant) has been significantly reduced because modern farming methods have depleted the soil of this mineral. The body's elimination system therefore has to work harder than ever to deal with this level of pollutants. And while the work it has to do has increased, the support it's getting in terms of antioxidants and enzymes has declined.

## An overburdened system

When the elimination system is unable to handle its workload effectively it has no choice but to store waste products that should be removed from the body in body tissue such as the colon and the liver. This extra burden creates even more strain on the elimination system, making it less effective at dealing with its day-to-day work. In this way a continuous cycle is created that ultimately results in a decline in health and well-being. In Chapters Five, Six and Seven you will find a deeper analysis of how the elimination system works, and how overburdening can result in poor health. Another factor that can overburden the elimination system is a food intolerance problem, and this is discussed in depth in the following chapter.

It's not just the intake of toxins that creates problems for the body's elimination system; the average modern diet also makes the elimination system work extremely hard. The questions in the following Lifestyle Challenge will help you assess your current diet and lifestyle.

## Lifestyle Challenge

1   I eat 'ready meals' at least three times a week   **yes/no**
2   I drink at least 1½ litres/2½ pints/1½ quarts water a day   **yes/no**
3   I like salty foods and usually sprinkle salt on my meals   **yes/no**
4   I buy organic produce whenever possible   **yes/no**
5   I drink two or more cups of coffee a day   **yes/no**
6   I eat at least two pieces of fruit a day   **yes/no**
7   I drink two or more cups of tea a day   **yes/no**
8   I eat two or three portions of vegetables a day   **yes/no**
9   I like sugary foods and eat them often   **yes/no**
10   I take regular exercise at least three times a week   **yes/no**
11   I eat takeaways at least once a week   **yes/no**
12   I regularly practise meditation or relaxation techniques   **yes/no**
13   Most days I will have at least one alcoholic drink   **yes/no**
14   I go out of my way to avoid processed foods   **yes/no**
15   I regularly drink cola and other fizzy drinks   **yes/no**
16   I eat meat no more than three times a week   **yes/no**
17   I frequently eat processed meats (eg ham, salami)   **yes/no**
18   I manage the stress and pressure in my life very well   **yes/no**
19   I often eat diet products (low-cal colas, cakes, etc)   **yes/no**
20   I eat breakfast and regular meals throughout the day   **yes/no**
21   I take headache tablets quite frequently   **yes/no**
22   I rarely eat fried foods   **yes/no**
23   I use non-prescription medication frequently   **yes/no**
24   I avoid using vegetable spreads   **yes/no**
25   I regularly eat refined foods like white bread and white rice   **yes/no**

**Score one point for each 'yes' to an odd-numbered question**
**Score one point for each 'no' to even-numbered question**

**Total Score**


A score of 12 or above suggests your current lifestyle and dietary habits may be over-burdening your elimination system, and it's also likely that you are experiencing a range of minor health problems such as lack of energy or frequent colds and infections. As I've already mentioned, the average diet and lifestyle doesn't do a great deal to support our health and well-being. It's time to break the cycle and stop living at the lower end of the health spectrum.

## Breaking the cycle

Detoxing is a way of breaking the cycle – it allows the elimination system and the body as a whole to rebalance and strengthen itself. In essence, a detox involves two basic steps.

**Step One** is to lighten the amount of work the body's elimination system needs to do. This means avoiding foods that are highly refined, sugar-loaded and full of unhealthy chemicals and fats. It also means avoiding stimulants and alcohol that put additional strain on the digestive system and the liver (more on this later). A food intolerance condition also adds extra burden to the elimination system, so you will also need to avoid trigger foods at the same time as supporting and strengthening the elimination system. During the Super Energy Detox you will be eating foods that are easy for the elimination system to assimilate – this will allow the system to relax a little and work on removing unwanted stored materials.

**Step Two** is to support the elimination system while it's doing the cleansing work, which means keeping to a diet that helps create the right environment for this to happen. Simple steps such as eating alkaline-forming foods and drinking plenty of water will greatly help this process, so too will practising energy exercises such as belly breathing (page 92) and taking specific natural supplements (page 61).

## chapter 4

# Food Intolerance

Food intolerance is a relatively common condition, but because it's so difficult to diagnose many people can have it for years without being aware of it. Intolerance is not the same thing as a food allergy, which provokes acute and immediate symptoms that can be life-threatening. Food intolerance provokes delayed reactions that can take up to three or four days to manifest themselves. It is associated with a diverse range of chronic (rather than acute) symptoms that are highly detrimental to overall well-being, but are not life threatening.

It is common for people who have food intolerance to feel under the weather a lot, or to feel overly tired for no apparent reason. Intolerance can also have a detrimental influence on your mental and emotional state, and is often associated with mild depression or brain fog (an inability to concentrate properly), joint aches and pains, digestive disturbance and migraines, keeping sufferers in the low-to-middle region of the health spectrum.

Food intolerance is highly disruptive to all the body's different elimination channels, and most sufferers are acutely aware of the impact it has on their digestive systems. The condition also puts extra strain on the other channels, including the liver, lymphatic system and kidneys, and this results in the whole elimination system becoming overburdened.

Ironically, when the elimination system is overburdened, it perpetuates the conditions for further food intolerance problems to develop and so creates a vicious circle. For many people intolerance can develop because their elimination system has previously been overburdened due to other dietary and lifestyle factors (see below).

The Super Energy Detox is particularly beneficial if you have a food intolerance problem, because it excludes the major culprit foods that are known to provoke intolerance. By avoiding suspect foods for a period of time, you will give your body the opportunity to stabilize and strengthen and you will be following dietary and lifestyle strategies that support and re-balance the individual elimination channels. You will also be introduced to specific nutritional supplements that are useful for healing the underlying body systems that are often involved with a food intolerance condition.

## Is it possible you have intolerance?

Answer the questions below to help find out.

### Food Intolerance Indicator

1  My abdomen feels bloated a lot of the time  **yes/no**
2  I have flatulence (wind) or indigestion a lot  **yes/no**
3  I get constipation and/or diarrhoea regularly  **yes/no**
4  I frequently have a blocked or runny nose  **yes/no**
5  My energy levels can fluctuate widely throughout the day  **yes/no**
6  I get headaches or migraines quite a lot  **yes/no**
7  I feel tired even though I've had enough sleep  **yes/no**
8  I have eczema, acne or a similar skin condition  **yes/no**
9  My joints often feel stiff and my muscles often ache  **yes/no**
10  I get fluid retention (swollen face, ankles, hands)  **yes/no**
11  My weight can fluctuate up and down for no obvious reason  **yes/no**
12  I find it difficult to lose weight even when counting calories  **yes/no**
13  I crave certain foods or drinks  **yes/no**
14  I can sometimes binge on certain foods  **yes/no**
15  I can feel excessively tired after eating  **yes/no**

**Score one point for each 'yes'**

**Total Score**

If you have answered 'yes' to at least eight questions, it's possible you are suffering with food intolerance. The steps you need to take to investigate this further and then deal with this condition are outlined later in this chapter, but first let's take a look at what can provoke the problem.

## What causes food intolerance

Scientists who work in this field are unable to fully explain the reasons why food intolerance develops, but the general consensus is that eating the same food over and over again is in part responsible for creating the conditions that cause the problem. This argument seems logical, given that the main culprit foods are those that are eaten frequently in the West. Wheat is a good example, because it's a food often associated with intolerance. It's not uncommon to eat wheat for breakfast (cereal), lunch (sandwich) and dinner (pasta or pizza) as well as for snacks in between (biscuits, cookies, pretzels, etc). Cow's milk products are also a common trigger food and they're eaten regularly too, while corn is a favourite culprit in North America as it is found in many processed foods.

Most food intolerance conditions are usually associated with some form of digestive disturbance, ranging from mild symptoms such as bloating through to debilitating complaints like frequent diarrhoea. While symptoms vary from person to person, there appears to be an association between wheat (and the other gluten grains) and the more disruptive digestive problems. Intolerance to dairy products is more often associated with respiratory problems, such as asthma and a constant runny nose, and skin conditions like eczema.

The most common intolerance offenders are listed in the following chart (in no particular order); these foods can be difficult to digest properly if the elimination system is overburdened. However, it should be noted that an individual can develop an intolerance to any food, not just those listed opposite.

| Main Food Intolerance Culprits | Other Common Culprits |
| --- | --- |
| Wheat | Eggs |
| Other gluten grains (oats, barley, rye) | Soya produce |
| Dairy products | Citrus fruits (not lemons) |
| Yeast | Nightshade food family, eg. |
| Sugar |   tomatoes, aubergines (eggplants) |
| Corn (mainly in North America) |   potatoes and peppers |
| Alcohol | |

## A two-way relationship

The predominant paradigm used in medicine is the concept of 'host resistance'. This theory provides us with a model to understand why two people can come into contact with a cold virus say, but only one will actually catch a cold. The person who doesn't catch it may already have acquired resistance to this particular virus or have a robust immune system that stops the virus from taking hold in the body, whereas the person who catches the cold may be run down or tired, which means their immune system is less resilient.

Host resistance can also be used to shed light on the problem of food intolerance. What this concept tells us is that it isn't simply that a particular food is inherently bad. A great many people regularly eat the major culprit foods listed in the table above with no problems whatsoever. What is important *is the relationship between the food and the individual*. It is this two-way process that results in a certain food provoking an intolerance condition.

In some instances food intolerance may be due to an inherited predisposition that results in your being unable to correctly digest and assimilate a certain food, but in a great many other cases the development of food intolerance can signal an underlying imbalance with the body's elimination system – this is especially the case with the functioning of the digestive tract. Modern lifestyles – what we eat, how we live, exercise, work and manage our emotions – do not generally create the ideal conditions for the digestive tract (and the whole elimination system) to function at its best.

This is particularly true of the majority of processed foods which are often high in sugar, salt and additives, yet low in dietary fibre and nutrients. These foods don't support the functioning of the digestive tract and they can create the conditions for a leaky gut to develop – especially if other contributory factors such as antibiotic use are involved. When the gut has become too permeable (leaky), molecules that should be eliminated from the body, such as partially digested protein molecules or chemical toxins, are able to cross the gut wall into the bloodstream and intercellular fluid. Once in the blood and body fluids, these molecules are treated as foreign invaders, triggering an immune response that is behind many of the symptoms that sufferers of food intolerance experience. (See the next chapter for a deeper review of how the digestive system functions.)

The fact that food intolerance may be caused by diet and lifestyle should be viewed as good news, because it means that intolerance need not be a long-term condition. When the correct steps are taken to improve the functioning of the digestive tract, support the whole elimination system and rebalance the body, the susceptibility to react to certain foods usually reduces. This is where the Super Energy Detox comes in, because it offers a step-by-step approach for strengthening these underlying bodily functions. After taking these steps, many people find they can re-introduce a problem food in moderate quantities with no adverse reaction.

## Is yeast a part of your problem?

Quite often, people who are intolerant to the major culprit foods such as wheat and dairy also have a sensitivity to things with yeast in them, like bread and alcohol. In fact, in many cases, it is actually the existence of the yeast sensitivity that helps create the conditions for the food intolerance to develop. Yeast sensitivity is associated with a number of specific symptoms. To find out whether you may have this condition, answer the following questions.

## Yeast Sensitivity Indicator

1  I get a lot of flatulence (wind)  **yes/no**
2  My abdomen feels bloated most of the time  **yes/no**
3  My bowel function can be irregular (constipation/diarrhoea)  **yes/no**
4  I sometimes suffer from 'brain fog'  **yes/no**
5  I've suffered with vaginal thrush more than once  **yes/no**
6  I crave sugary foods  **yes/no**
7  I crave yeast-containing foods like bread  **yes/no**
8  A short exposure to household chemicals makes me feel bad  **yes/no**
9  Drinking a small quantity of alcohol can give me a hangover  **yes/no**
10  My symptoms can get worse when I'm in a damp building  **yes/no**
11  I regularly drink alcohol (or have in the past)  **yes/no**
12  I am on the contraceptive pill (or have been in the past)  **yes/no**
13  I've had at least 3 courses of antibiotics in the past few years  **yes/no**
14  My symptoms get better when I'm in a warm, dry climate  **yes/no**
15  I've had a lot of stress over the past few years  **yes/no**
16  My energy levels fluctuate frequently  **yes/no**
17  I get mood swings quite frequently  **yes/no**
18  I suffer with pre-menstrual symptoms  **yes/no**

**Score one point for each 'yes'**

**Total Score**

A score of at least eight suggests there is a possibility you are sensitive to foods containing yeast. A score of twelve or more is a strong indication that you have a yeast problem. Key indicators that can help you assess this situation more clearly are whether you have answered yes to questions 5–10. Questions 11–13 are factors known to contribute to yeast sensitivity.

If you scored eight or above, follow the guidelines for yeast sensitivity in Chapter Fourteen while you are following the detox programme, because you should avoid specific foods in order not to make the condition worse. Most of these foods (like refined sugar and alcohol) do not play a part on the detox programme anyway, but there are a few 'healthy' foods allowed on the programme that you should avoid if you scored highly on this test.

Reaction to yeast-containing foods tends to occur when the digestive tract is not functioning up to par. We all have a certain amount of yeast in our digestive tracts, it's only when the yeast multiplies to an excessive level that yeast sensitivity can develop, and the only way this can occur is when there is a disruption and depletion of the mechanisms that support the health of the gut. These mechanisms include the role of the friendly bacteria that reside in the intestines (page 32) and the specific antibodies that fend off foreign invaders. The health of the delicate mucus lining of the gut wall is also important.

The health of the gut's protective mechanisms is extremely vulnerable to the influence of diet, alcohol, lifestyle and the use of pharmaceutical drugs such as antibiotics. A lack of gut flora, a disruption of the mucus lining of the gut wall and an excess of intestinal yeast create the ideal conditions for increased intestinal permeability, or leaky gut. This condition can then provoke intolerance to other foods such as wheat or dairy products.

The Super Energy Detox is a useful first step to dealing with yeast sensitivity, but you should take additional steps after the detox if you want to deal with this condition effectively. The maintenance programme will be highly beneficial, but I also recommend you consult a nutritionist for some professional support, and that you read some of the many excellent books available on this specific topic.

## Overcoming food intolerance – a step-by-step approach

The Super Energy Detox offers a step-by-step approach for dealing with a food intolerance condition, but the first thing you need to do is determine whether your symptoms are definitely related to food intolerance. This includes identifying the particular foods that are associated with your symptoms.

Food intolerance can be a tricky thing to identify. The questionnaire on page 21 can only give you an *indication* that you have an intolerance problem – it can't *confirm* whether or not this is the case. In fact, an affirmative response to many of the questions in the food intolerance indicator may simply show that your elimination system is overburdened and struggling to perform its work rather than a true food intolerance condition. If it is the case that your body's elimination system is simply working too hard, this should be viewed as good news, because it means that the detox programme will help you rebalance this system, which should result in improvements to your overall well-being.

To assess your situation in a deeper way you can do one of three things. First, you could have a biochemical test for food intolerance. There are plenty of these tests available on the market, but not all of them provide accurate results. One of the best is the ELISA test, but it is relatively expensive. It can be worthwhile consulting a nutritionist, who can arrange for biochemical tests to assess food intolerance, yeast sensitivity and intestinal permeability (leaky gut). See page 257 for details on locating a nutritionist.

Your second option is to conduct an elimination trial. This involves avoiding any potential culprit foods for a period of two weeks while continuing with your usual day-to-day activities (i.e. making no other changes to your diet and lifestyle). Conducted correctly, an elimination trial will probably provide you with more accurate information than a biochemical test. This is because the body's response to removing a particular food is the clearest indicator of whether or not this food is provoking any symptoms. Full instructions for conducting an elimination trial are given in Appendix Four (page 245).

Your third option is to use the Super Energy Detox as an alternative elimination trial, because during the three weeks it excludes all the main food intolerance culprits – wheat, oats, barley, rye, dairy produce, sugar, yeast, alcohol and citrus. Using the detox as a method of assessing intolerance can be inaccurate, however, because during this time you'll also be making many other changes to your eating habits and lifestyle and this will make it difficult to assess whether any changes to your well-being are directly associated with removing a culprit food or with the other changes you've made.

The Super Energy Detox consists of two elements. The first is the three-week detox. This part of the programme can be beneficial to anyone, regardless of whether food intolerance is present. During the detox, wheat and the other gluten grains, dairy produce, sugar, yeast and alcohol are all avoided. The reason for excluding these foods is not merely because they are common intolerance culprits, it's because they conflict with the underlying dietary principles that need to be followed if you are going to help the body cleanse itself (page 47). This is why stimulants (e.g. coffee, tea and cola) and all refined and processed foods are also avoided.

You will also use specific nutritional strategies to help your body's elimination system rebalance and strengthen itself. These include natural approaches for dealing with leaky gut, a condition often associated with intolerance as I've mentioned already. Working to strengthen the body's elimination system is an important step if an intolerance condition is to be dealt with properly.

The three-week detox period is not long enough to deal with a food intolerance problem adequately. Thus the second stage of the programme is the maintenance phase, which is specifically for those who have intolerance. It lasts from two to four months. One aspect of this stage is that it is necessary to avoid your culprit foods throughout this period.

*If you use the detox as a method of determining whether you may have intolerance, it's very important to follow the instructions for re-testing suspect foods in Chapter Seventeen before starting the maintenance programme.* The reason for this is that there is absolutely no value in removing a certain food from your diet for a period of two to four months unless you know you are experiencing a genuine intolerance to that food. The reintroduction test given in Chapter Seventeen will help you determine whether or not this is the case. Many food intolerance sufferers find that after avoiding the culprit food for this length of time and simultaneously taking steps to address the underlying body conditions, they are then able to reintroduce moderate quantities of the offending food with no adverse reaction.

So far, several references have been made to the body's elimination system. Working with this system – the digestive tract, liver, kidneys, lymphatic system, skin and lungs – is a key part of the detox programme, so it's useful to understand the function of each of the individual components. Let's start by having a look at the digestive system.

## chapter 5

# The Digestive System

## The importance of the digestive system

As a profession, nutritionists are somewhat obsessed with the health of the digestive system. People come to us for help with a diverse range of complaints, from joint pains and skin problems to depression and pre-menstrual tension, but each one will be faced with the same in-depth questioning about their bowel function!

On the face of it this might appear strange, but there is a strong link between how well the digestive system is functioning and the health of the body. For example, a common complaint such as chronic constipation is directly associated with increased risk of numerous diseases, including heart disease, gallstones and colorectal cancer (the latter is currently the third leading cause of cancer death). Looking after your digestive system is therefore good preventative medicine that will help reduce the risk of your getting more serious complaints.

The digestive tract is one of the body's most important cleansing and elimination channels. If it's not performing its job adequately it creates a great deal of extra pressure on the other elimination channels, which in turn can lead to poor health. This is especially true of the liver which, as discussed in the next chapter, works closely alongside the digestive system.

It is through the processes of digestion and absorption that we obtain all the nutrients from food. You've probably heard the phrase 'you are what you eat', but a more accurate description is actually 'you are what you absorb'. Most people's diets aren't adequate for their nutritional needs, and this is reflected in several government-funded studies showing that vitamin and mineral deficiencies are commonplace. However, even the healthiest, nutrient-rich diet will be of little benefit if the digestive system is unable to absorb the nutrients. Factors that affect the ability to absorb and utilise nutrients include depleted digestive enzymes and disrupted gut flora, and both of these conditions are quite common.

## The link with food intolerance

Food intolerance can be associated with many digestive complaints, including bloating, indigestion, heartburn, constipation, diarrhoea and flatulence, and these represent a classic 'chicken or egg' situation. As I mentioned in the previous chapter, an overburdened digestive system often creates the conditions for food intolerance to occur, then, once the intolerance has developed, continuing to eat the offending food perpetuates the cycle.

The mechanisms by which intolerance causes digestive complaints can vary according to both the particular food and the person. Sensitivity to yeast-containing foods may develop when there is an excessive amount of yeast in the lower part of the digestive tract, and this is usually accompanied by a deficiency in the healthy, friendly bacteria that are supposed to populate this region. An excess of yeast and a lack of friendly bacteria in turn increase the risk of leaky gut, which then increases the risk of developing intolerance to other foods.

Fluid retention (oedema) is a condition often associated with leaky gut. The excess water that is held in the cells and body tissues is there for a purpose. The body needs to be maintained at a specific alkaline level in order for vital bodily functions to perform normally. The unwanted molecules that seep through the gut wall into the body fluids are acidic, therefore the body is protecting itself from the potential damage they can cause by bathing them in excess cellular fluid (see Chapter Seven for more details on this point).

For some people, intolerance may be provoked by a lack of digestive enzymes (see opposite), which means that food progresses through the digestive tract in a partially digested state and may irritate the lining of the gut wall. In some instances, it is the food itself that irritates the digestive tract and disrupts the gut flora and mucosa of the intestinal wall. In both cases, the risk of leaky gut is perpetuated.

The good news is that there are lots of simple steps you can take to improve the overall health of your digestive system. The Super Energy Detox includes specific foods and natural supplements that are known to enhance digestive function and help with leaky gut. These in turn will help to deal with a food intolerance problem.

## Understanding the digestive system

Digestion and absorption are complicated and delicate processes. Briefly, this is what happens.

The first phase is the action of chewing, which stimulates the production of digestive enzymes in the stomach and small intestine. Protein digestion starts in the acid environment of the stomach and specific digestive enzymes are required for this process to be completed adequately. These can only be manufactured when there are sufficient supplies of specific vitamins and minerals, especially vitamin B6 and zinc.

Next, the pancreas and the small intestine together produce a further set of digestive enzymes that are alkaline. There are specific enzymes to work with fat, carbohydrate and protein foods. The liver also gets involved by producing bile that breaks down fatty foods before the enzymes act on them. Once the food has been broken down into its constituent molecular parts, it can be absorbed into the bloodstream or lymph. About 90 per cent of the nutrients we absorb are received through the wall of the small intestine; the remaining 10 per cent are absorbed through the large intestine. Water is reabsorbed through the large intestine wall along with sodium and certain vitamins.

If there is an inadequate supply of digestive enzymes in either the stomach or small intestine, food will progress through the digestive tract in a partially-digested state, resulting in poor absorption and utilization of nutrients, which increases the likelihood of vitamin and mineral deficiencies. It can also provoke digestive problems and, as I have mentioned before, contribute to the development of food intolerance.

There are several factors that can disrupt the production of digestive enzymes. Emotional stress and worry can deplete them, as can excessive consumption of coffee, tea and alcohol. Eating quickly or skipping meals also puts a strain on the body's enzyme systems – see Chapters Nine and Ten for more on this.

Unabsorbed food molecules continue their journey through the small intestine and progress into the large intestine (colon). Sufficient dietary fibre (the indigestible portion of grains, vegetables and fruits) is essential if the colon is to function properly, because fibre promotes the action of peristalsis, the wave-like motions of the intestines. Unfortunately, the average Western diet is high in refined foods and doesn't provide adequate levels of dietary fibre – this is one reason why constipation is so commonplace. Furthermore, not all fibre is the same. Certain foods, such as vegetables and oats, provide fibre in a form that has a gentle action on the digestive system, while other foods (such as the bran portion of wheat) can have a highly irritating effect on the colon, often perpetuating constipation rather than alleviating it.

Another essential component required by the colon is adequate fluid intake. When there is insufficient fluid, peristalsis is made much harder and the effectiveness of this elimination channel is reduced.

Cellular wastes such as worn-out cells, deactivated hormones and cholesterol, and exogenous toxins like pharmaceutical drugs, are transported from the liver via bile into the intestines so they can be eliminated from the body, but if the digestive tract is not functioning up to par these toxic wastes cannot be removed effectively. This then starts to put more strain on the other elimination channels and perpetuates a condition where the body as a whole becomes overloaded with toxins. This is why ensuring that the digestive tract is performing its elimination duties properly is one of the most important principles of the detox programme.

## Some helpful friends

Over the millennia we humans have formed a good relationship with the bacteria that live in our gut. We provide them with a good home and, as long as we look after them by choosing the right type of diet and lifestyle, they repay us ten-fold.

Our friendly bacteria perform a number of important tasks: they help break down the toxins that have been transported to the colon in the bile by the liver (if there were insufficient bacteria, there would be an increased risk of these substances being reabsorbed back into the body via the colon wall); they also help break down cholesterol (also eliminated via bile), protecting your cardiovascular system and reducing your risk of gallstones. In addition, they produce B vitamins (especially B6, B3, folic acid and biotin) and vitamin K. Last, but by no means least, they are vital for maintaining the healthy functioning of the gut wall.

The intestines can be viewed as a complex internal eco-system. There are several different strains of gut flora and it is important to maintain the right balance between them if we want our digestive system to be in tip-top working order and to support our overall health. The intestines of a healthy person should contain about 1.5kg/3lb of friendly bacteria, but for the majority of people this simply isn't the case. Gut flora is quite delicate and can be easily depleted. Poor diet, stress, alcohol, drugs and problems in other parts of the digestive system (eg. lack of digestive enzymes in the stomach and small intestine) are just some of the factors that create the conditions for an imbalance in this internal colony.

Antibiotics are most detrimental to our resident bacteria. They disrupt the flora in the gut as well as the bacteria that reside elsewhere on and in the body (the genito-urinary tract, skin, mouth and nose for example). An antibiotic is a powerful drug designed to kill a bacterial infection, but the way it works can be likened to the action of a nuclear bomb. The drug can't differentiate between the bad guys (the bacterial invader that can cause disease) and the good guys (the bacteria that naturally live in the body and promote health), so it nukes the whole lot.

When the friendly bacteria have been depleted it paves the way for other residents in the body, such as yeast, to proliferate. This is why, after taking a course of antibiotics, it's not uncommon to get thrush (an excess of yeast in the vagina) and digestive complaints like irritable bowel syndrome. Antibiotics may be necessary from time to time, but it is important to replace your friendly bacteria afterwards, and you can do this by eating live yogurt and by taking a good-quality probiotic supplement. Other substances which disrupt your friendly bacteria include steroid drugs (which includes the pill) and smoking. Stress also has a strong negative influence on the health of these bacteria.

Your diet plays a key role in the internal eco-system equation. Lots of complex carbohydrates, moderate amounts of easily digested proteins and limited amounts of fat and sugar will promote the presence of the good friendly bacteria that perform the health-promoting functions outlined above (the bifido strains). Conversely, a diet high in protein, fat, sugar and alcohol will increase the population of the not-so-beneficial strains of bacteria (the bacteroids) as well as yeast. When these different strains of gut flora become unbalanced and when there is an excess of yeast, there is an increased risk of digestive problems, leaky gut and food intolerance.

As the digestive system is such an important elimination channel, many of the key principles of the Super Energy Detox are designed to support and strengthen it. You will be introduced to a number of wonderful foods that can help heal and rejuvenate the digestive tract, plus several nutritional cleansing supplements that work directly with your digestive system.

## chapter 6

# The Liver

## The importance of the liver

Unlike many other organs, the liver performs its work silently. It doesn't pump like the heart, we don't notice it gurgling and rumbling like the digestive system, and it doesn't have any way of telling us it's under pressure – and yet it performs a mind-boggling range of vital bodily tasks and is one of our most important cleansing channels. As modern diet and lifestyle are putting an increasing strain on this organ, working with the liver is a key component of the detox programme.

The health of your liver, like that of your digestive system, has an important impact on your overall health and well-being. There are several complaints that are directly related to how well the liver is performing. Heart disease, obesity, pre-menstrual tension and menopausal symptoms are just a few of the conditions that can be made worse if your liver is overloaded and so unable to perform its work efficiently. Frequent fatigue, indigestion, difficulty in digesting fatty foods and poor skin are some of the signs that suggest this organ is under pressure and could benefit from a detox programme. Let's take a brief look at some of the functions that this amazing organ performs.

## The functions of the liver

Without a liver we simply couldn't use the nutrients we get from our food. It is directly involved in the digestion and metabolism of proteins, carbohydrates and fats. Protein foods are required for cellular repair and the production of hormones, and it is the liver that converts digested protein molecules (amino acids) into a form that the body can use. This conversion process creates toxic metabolic by-products (namely ammonia) that the liver converts into a less toxic substance (urea) to be eliminated from the body.

Carbohydrate foods such as grains, fruits and sugar need to be converted into the body's favourite energy source, glucose. The liver has a role in converting certain carbohydrates into glucose (for example, it converts fruit sugar or fructose into glucose); it also plays a vital role in the overall management of blood sugar levels. Maintaining the right levels of blood glucose is extremely important – it's necessary to have stable blood glucose in order to have energy to go about your daily activities. It's also an important factor in keeping your emotions even and balanced. Food intolerance is often associated with difficulty in keeping blood sugar levels stable, which provokes symptoms such as energy slumps at different points during the day (see Chapter Seventeen for more on this point).

Prompted by insulin and glucagon from the pancreas, your liver controls how much glucose is circulating in your blood. When there is an excess, say after eating a piece of chocolate cake, the liver removes it and converts it into glycogen which gets stored in muscle tissue or in the cells of the liver itself. If the receptor sites for glycogen storage are full, it then converts glucose into triacylglycerol (fat) that can be stored in adipose tissue. This is the process by which a piece of chocolate cake ends up on your hips. When glucose levels fall too low, for example after strenuous activity or skipping a meal, the liver reconverts its glycogen stores back into glucose, providing you with energy.

The liver also produces bile, an alkaline liquid that is stored in the gall bladder. Foods containing fat are emulsified by the action of bile before being acted upon by the pancreatic enzymes. Bile also acts as the carrier fluid for removing foreign toxins, deactivated hormones, cholesterol and cellular debris (eg. worn-out blood cells) from the body after the liver has processed them.

## The chemical factory

The liver is the major organ for metabolizing foreign chemical substances like alcohol, drugs, environmental toxins and additives found in food. It converts them into harmless water-soluble metabolites that can then be excreted via the digestive tract or the kidneys. It also deals with internal 'chemicals' by deactivating used hormones such as oestrogen, thyroxin and adrenaline. The process of metabolism creates a large amount of waste products that the liver also processes, and all of these substances are passed into bile for excretion.

If the liver is overloaded, its ability to deactivate these hormones is impaired. Take the case of adrenaline – our 'get up and go' hormone. Adrenaline is released early in the morning so we feel wide awake and ready to take on the challenges of the day, but each time we feel stressed the body also releases additional adrenaline, making us alert and giving us energy to deal with the problem provoking the emotional response. After the crisis is over, if the liver is functioning properly it will process the hormone so that it can be eliminated from the body. We then feel relaxed and calm again. If the liver is unable to deactivate adrenaline efficiently, however, it will circulate in the bloodstream for longer than necessary, making us feel jittery and hyper or unable to sleep when we go to bed. The same thing happens with caffeine, a chemical which your liver finds quite hard work to process. If your liver is unable to deactivate caffeine, you can't get to sleep at night.

Although most of us are aware of the effects of too much adrenaline or caffeine, we don't necessarily notice the effect of our livers being unable to process other chemicals. This is bad news, because an overloaded liver that is unable to do its work effectively increases the risk of disease. If not safely deactivated, the chemical compounds found in environmental toxins and metabolic processes (and those produced by the liver itself in the natural course of its work) can cause serious damage to the body, including damage to DNA.

Leaky gut puts a great deal of additional strain on the liver. The partially digested food molecules, chemical toxins and other unwanted materials that are able to seep through the gut wall and enter body fluids and the bloodstream need to be worked on by the liver, so those with food intolerance (which is usually associated with leaky gut) will usually also have an overburdened liver. The diet and nutritional cleansing supplements used in this detox programme are designed to support liver function, which in turn will also help deal with an intolerance condition.

The liver acts as a storage site for various useful substances, including glycogen (a source of energy), the fat-soluble vitamins A, D, E and K and certain B vitamins, plus the minerals iron and copper. The liver will also store toxic material if the body's cleansing channels as a whole are overloaded and unable to remove them effectively (when the digestive system is sluggish, for example). It is safer for the body to have these chemicals tucked away within the confines of the liver than circulating in the bloodstream where they can cause damage (the other main storage site for toxic substances is adipose tissue or fat), but they do create additional strain on the liver. It may be a highly resilient organ, but an on-going accumulation of chemicals over the long term is bound to take its toll and affect its ability to function.

## Helping the liver

This brief overview of the liver's functions has highlighted the importance of looking after this organ. The Super Energy Detox is designed to support your liver, and it does this by recommending foods that are good for it and by adding a selection of natural foods and herbs that have been found to have health-promoting benefits for this organ. You will find out about these particular foods and herbs in Chapter Ten. Here are a few other suggestions for keeping your liver functioning at its best. One of the best things we can do is simply reduce our exposure to substances that the liver finds toxic and has difficulty processing. Taking steps such as buying organic produce and avoiding refined and processed foods is very helpful because it lightens the liver's chemical load.

Try not to give your liver extra work when you can easily avoid it. Alcohol is seen as hard work by the liver, so you should aim to keep alcohol intake low. Wine can contain a cocktail of chemical additives (including sulphites that are very toxic to the liver), so if you drink wine, choose organic if possible – at least with organic versions you are avoiding added chemical stress. Also, don't be too hasty in taking over-the-counter medicines, because these too contain strong chemicals that the liver has to deactivate. Before reaching for the painkillers, try taking some natural steps to rebalance yourself (in Chapter Fifteen there is a quick headache relief massage that is usually highly effective).

To have a healthy liver and to support your overall health you need a balanced diet consisting of the right combination of carbohydrates, proteins and fats. Refined carbohydrates (high-sugar and processed foods) dump excessive amounts of glucose into the bloodstream which need to be removed and converted by the liver, whereas complex carbohydrates (such as whole grains and pulses) are much easier on the liver because they release their energy potential at a slow rate. Complex carbohydrates also support your health in a number of other ways and tend to be a good source of the B vitamins that are essential to your liver's proper functioning.

Protein is an essential component of a healthy diet, but an excess will put strain on your liver. Generally, two servings of good-quality protein a day will meet most requirements, and they should be low in saturated fat. Dietary fats perform numerous important bodily functions and they're essential for good health, so it's important to have a small amount of healthy fats every day. The healthy fats that support your liver include oily fish, cold pressed vegetable oils (olive, sunflower and sesame), nuts and seeds. Avoid saturated fats and do not use butter, oils or nuts that have become rancid or hydrogenated.

The liver loves vitamin C, so a diet high in fresh fruits and green vegetables is highly beneficial. It also loves sulphur-containing foods, because it uses sulphur when it's deactivating unwanted compounds. Onions, garlic, leeks and the cruciferous vegetables (broccoli, cauliflower, cabbage, kale and Brussels sprouts) are all good sources of sulphur. Both vitamin C and sulphur are used as natural cleansing substances to assist the liver during the detox programme.

## chapter 7

# The Other Channels

In this chapter we will look at the remaining four elimination channels – the kidneys, lymph, lungs and skin. Each of these has an important role to play in maintaining the integrity of the body's cleansing mechanisms and in our overall health. The Super Energy Detox includes lots of straightforward nutritional and lifestyle strategies that support the functioning of these four channels. They are introduced in Chapter Ten and during each week of the programme.

## The kidneys

The main role of the kidneys is to filter out impurities from the blood – 1 litre/1 quart blood is filtered through the kidneys each and every minute of the day. Substances that the body needs, such as glucose, proteins and mineral salts, are readily reabsorbed back into the blood, while molecules that the body definitely doesn't want, including waste products produced by the cells during metabolism and any other toxic substances, are removed and eliminated in urine. Blood and body fluids need to be kept within a specific alkaline range (7.35–7.45Ph) in order for the cells to function at their best, and it is the kidney's job (along with the lungs) to ensure that this range is maintained.

Metabolism – the process of utilizing nutrients from food – happens at a cellular level and creates by-products known as metabolic ash. Each cell of the body is like a small furnace that has to burn nutrients to release its intrinsic components. During this process the furnace produces residues similar to the ash that is left behind after burning logs in a fire, and these need to be removed from cellular fluid and the bloodstream. This is where the kidneys come in.

Metabolic ash has a specific level of acidity or alkalinity depending on the type of food that has been eaten. An acidic ash is produced when protein foods and most grains are metabolized, while vegetables and fruits produce an alkaline ash. (Interestingly, this is not associated with the actual acidity of the food – lemons, for example, produce an alkaline ash when metabolized.)

Cellular fluid and blood are maintained at an alkaline level. Acidic ash can disrupt this balance if it is not removed, and it is also potentially dangerous because it can cause damage to cells and vital bodily functions. Buffering systems have been designed to safely transport acidic residues from the body by 'coating' the acid ash molecules with alkaline molecules such as calcium. In other words, each time meat (or other acid-forming foods) is eaten, the body utilizes the available calcium reserves to remove metabolic wastes. The minerals potassium and sodium are also used in this process.

An excess of acid-forming foods such as meat, cheese and bread puts a great deal of strain on the kidneys and the buffering systems, so that in the long term a diet containing a high proportion of these foods is associated with a number of degenerative diseases, including osteoporosis (bone loss) that occurs as a result of the depletion of calcium from the body.

The water balance of the body is another job for the kidneys. An excess of acid-forming foods increases the likelihood of oedema (fluid retention). Every cell of the body contains fluid, but when the kidneys and buffering systems cannot process the volume of acid-forming foods the body has no choice other than to bathe these acidic molecules in large amounts of cellular fluid to stop them from damaging the cells. The same process occurs when oedema is associated with food intolerance and leaky gut. The unwanted molecules that seep through the gut wall are acidic and therefore need to be bathed with excess cellular fluid until they can be eliminated.

The average modern diet contains a high proportion of acid-forming foods – all protein foods are acid-forming as are most grains. For example, a typical day's menu might consist of coffee, cereal and an egg with toast for breakfast, a sandwich (such as cheese, tuna, ham or bacon) and a fizzy drink for lunch, then meat or fish with a small serving of vegetables for dinner, plus a few glasses of wine. Ninety per cent of this menu is acid-forming, while the vegetables provide the 10 per cent of alkaline foods. Sugar and stimulants also have an acid-forming effect.

A diet high in acid-forming foods will have a substantial impact on your mood. It can make you feel tense or irritable, and it dulls the body's communication system. Also, whenever we experience negative emotional states (anxiety, worry, tension, anger, irritability), a whole range of chemical reactions are produced, and these have a further acidifying effect on the body. So it's easy to see how this two-way connection can create an unproductive cycle. For example, the acid-forming effect of a traditional English breakfast leaves us feeling heavy and slightly hyper before we've even left home, then being already slightly agitated, we respond to any travel problems by getting stressed or irritated – then this in turn produces more acid-forming chemicals in the body. By the time we get to our destination we're already feeling exhausted, so we reach for a strong cup of coffee to perk us up, which is another acid-forming substance ... and so it goes on. It's not surprising that we feel completely depleted by the end of the day.

Switching your diet from mostly acid-forming to mainly alkaline-forming foods supports the ability of your kidneys to function at their best. More importantly, it also has great benefits for your overall health. Conditions such as fluid retention are often eradicated. The body uses up lots of energy processing acidic foods, but when we eat a greater quantity of alkaline-forming foods we liberate this energy to be used for other things. You may notice that you require less sleep, for example, and can achieve more with your day.

Most people also notice a significant difference in their mood after switching to an alkaline-forming diet – they feel calmer, more balanced and less upset by stress-provoking situations. The foods you will be eating on the Super Energy Detox are 70 to 80 per cent alkaline-forming and only 20 to 30 per cent acid-forming, which is practically the opposite of what many people are currently eating. Juicing, an integral part of the programme, is a great way of improving the acid-alkaline balance of the body and replenishing the nutrients required by the buffering systems.

# The lymphatic system

The lymphatic system performs a range of important functions that maintain the health of the body at cellular level. It consists of the spleen, thymus gland, bone marrow, lymph nodes and lymph fluid, and is responsible for producing many of the immune cells that protect us from infection. Every time you are fighting an infection – a cold, for example – your lymphatic system is spurred into action. The swelling in your neck is a sign that the lymph nodes are working hard to destroy the virus, and there are several other lymph nodes located in key areas of your body, including your armpits and pelvis.

Lymphatic fluid is particularly interesting. The pressure level of your cells is continually rising and falling. When it falls, fluid seeps from the bloodstream into the cells, then progresses into the lymphatic system to be cleaned and eventually restored to the bloodstream. There is a complex series of channels that move this lymph fluid around your body, an intricate network of capillaries and vessels that transports the fluid to the lymph nodes, which then remove any debris or foreign bacteria. These unwanted substances are subsequently eliminated from your body via the digestive tract and the cleaned lymph fluid eventually drains back into the bloodstream – where the whole process begins again (about 4 litres/4 quarts of intercellular lymph fluid are processed in this way each day).

Certain vitamins and minerals are important for the healthy functioning of the lymphatic system, and it is also important for the lymph fluid to be able to move through the vessels efficiently. After being worked on by the pancreas, liver and small intestine, dietary fat is absorbed through the small intestine into lymph fluid and then transported to the cells and bloodstream. Dietary fat is a difficult substance for the lymph system to transport, so eating a high-fat diet effectively clogs up the lymph channels, making the whole system less efficient. Insufficient fluid intake also affects the ability of the lymph system to do its job.

The cardiovascular system has the benefit of a heart to continuously pump blood through the veins and arteries, but the lymphatic system doesn't have such support. Instead, lymph fluid is pumped through the body by two processes: the action of breathing and the movement of muscles. A sedentary lifestyle and a pattern of shallow breathing can therefore result in the lymph system becoming stagnant. To support your lymph system and help prevent this happening, you will find both the physical exercises in Chapters Eight and Fourteen and the breathing exercises in Chapters Fourteen and Sixteen very useful.

## The lungs

The respiratory system works alongside the kidneys to maintain blood alkalinity; the lungs also operate as an elimination channel in their own right. About 500ml/2 cups fluid is excreted from the body every day via the lungs, and it can act as a carrier for eliminating volatile substances such as alcohol. As I mentioned earlier, the motion of breathing also supports the work of the lymphatic system so that, when we breathe properly, lymph fluid is pushed around the lymphatic system, encouraging cleansing. Deep and slow breathing also supports the digestive system by encouraging peristalsis.

Breathing exercises are an important part of the detox programme because they have such a valuable impact on the whole elimination system, but their benefits extend much further than this. Proper breathing has a positive effect on the health of the whole body, including the nervous system (involved in managing stress) and immune function.

## The skin

Your first defence against invading foreign bacteria is your skin, assisted by the friendly bacteria that live on it. Your skin also helps your body eliminate toxins when you sweat. Culturally we tend to be very against sweating, and so most people use antiperspirants, which usually contain harmful aluminium. Regular bathing should be enough to take care of personal hygiene issues without the use of antiperspirants, or you could use an aluminium-free deodorant that doesn't block the natural action of sweating.

Spotty skin is sometimes a reaction to airborne pollution and dirt, but the skin is also sometimes used as a storage site for toxins that can't be eliminated through other channels. In the philosophy of natural health,

storing toxins in the skin is considered better than storing these substances deeper in the body (such as in the vital organs or glands) where
they could do more damage. Spotty skin may be an indication of
an overburdened elimination system, and many natural health practitioners also believe that skin conditions such as eczema are associated
with a build-up of toxins within the body (although other conditions
such as food intolerance or a lack of essential fatty acids in the diet may
also be involved).

## chapter 8

# Getting Started

This chapter will provide you with an overview of the detox programme and highlight the key principles underpinning the detox. It lists the items you will need if you are going to get the best out of the detox, and introduces you to two important components of the programme – the energy exercises and lifestyle projects.

You will have the opportunity to personalize your programme according to your individual needs in Chapter Nine, and learn about specific cleansing supplements in Chapter Ten. Practical tips and guidelines on how to integrate the programme easily into your daily life are in Chapter Eleven, while Chapter Twelve discusses some of the common experiences people have during a detox and suggests strategies to deal with side effects. You will find it useful to read all these chapters before embarking on the programme.

## An overview

The detox programme lasts for three weeks, during which time you are encouraged to eat three meals and two snacks a day. You can determine your own portion sizes and eat as many fruits and vegetables as you like. If you are doing the programme when the weather is warm, follow the summer eating plan, which consists of a high proportion of raw foods such as fruits and salads. In the cold winter months you should follow the winter eating plan, which consists primarily of foods that have a warming and heating effect on the body, with raw foods kept to a minimum. (The reasons for providing you with summer and winter plans are discussed on page 79.)

**Week One** is a 'lighten your load' week in which you embark on a healthy eating plan (the reasons for this are in Chapter Twelve).

**Weeks Two and Three** involve eating mainly alkaline-forming foods and using specific natural supplements to help your body's cleansing activities.

There are lots of energy exercises and lifestyle projects for you to try each week.

## The key principles

There are seven key principles in the Super Energy Detox. Knowing what they are will help you understand the dietary guidelines you are about to follow.

### 1 Alkaline-forming foods

The average diet consists primarily of acid-forming food and drink – meat, fish, eggs, dairy produce, sugar, stimulants, alcohol and most grains such as wheat (the balance of alkaline-to-acid being often in the region of 20:80). As I have mentioned, a diet high in acid-forming foods puts strain on the whole elimination system (including the digestive system, liver, kidneys and lymph); it can deplete your energy levels and have a detrimental effect on your mood, and it also dulls the body's communication system.

The body prefers a diet that contains a high proportion of alkaline-forming foods, such as fruits, vegetables and juices, and it is essential to eat plenty of these foods during a detox, because they are the foods that create the best conditions for the body to cleanse itself. During Week One the balance of alkaline to acid is in the region of 50:50, then during Weeks Two and Three it is about 70 per cent alkaline to 30 per cent acid.

## 2 Antioxidant-rich foods

Antioxidants are always an extremely important part of our diets, but it is especially important to have a good supply during a detox because they help 'mop up' the stored unwanted wastes that your body is removing. You will be getting a whole spectrum of different antioxidants from the range of fruits, vegetables and seeds on the detox, and the daily vegetable juices will also provide an excellent source.

## 3 Energy foods

During the detox you are encouraged to eat foods that have a strong life force – foods that are fresh, have not been adulterated by chemicals and have not been processed or overcooked. When foods still contain their original energetic potential, they have a healing and rejuvenating effect on the body and a high nutritional (and enzyme) value. The concept of energy foods extends beyond nutrients, and the section on energy exercises on page 51 will expand on this concept.

## 4 Fibre-rich foods

Most of us don't get enough fibre, and the fibre we do eat (such as the insoluble fibre in wheat bran) can often be very irritating to the digestive tract. During the programme you will be eating lots of fruits and vegetables. These contain soluble fibre, which has a very gentle and healing effect on the digestive system and encourages it to remove impacted waste matter that has been stored in the colon. Fibre-rich foods also support the liver and are important for dealing with a food intolerance condition.

## 5 Balance

It is important to eat a balanced diet while detoxing, so that you get the full range of nutrients. Your carbohydrates are derived from fruits, vegetables and moderate levels of grains (including alkaline-forming grains such as millet). Protein foods include fish, nuts, seeds, yogurt and other vegetarian protein foods such as tofu (bean curd). Seeds also contain a good source of valuable antioxidants like zinc, plus essential fats that are important for liver function. You will also get dietary fats from oily fish, seeds and a small quantity of oil.

## 6 Water

Drinking lots of water is a very important part of the detox as it helps the elimination system while it is going through the cleansing process – water helps flush out toxins and keeps all the individual elimination channels working properly. The minimum amount of fluid required is 1½ litres/1½ quarts a day. This will replace what you lose through natural bodily processes (the kidneys, lungs and skin each lose at least 500ml/2 cups a day). It is important to drink water derived from a pure source, either bottled mineral water (not carbonated) or tap water that has been filtered to remove at least some of the unwanted substances such as heavy metals (lead, copper, aluminium).

## 7 Juices

Freshly prepared vegetable juices are an integral part of the programme because they support the body in numerous ways – they are highly alkaline-forming and are packed with antioxidant nutrients; they also contain high levels of enzymes, naturally occurring substances that have multiple health benefits. Juices are a high-energy, strong life-force food and a highly concentrated source of nutrition – a large glass of carrot juice, for example, takes nearly 500g/1lb carrots to make.

## Things you will need

Here is a list of non-food items you will need during the programme, not all of which are compulsory (those that are very important are marked with an asterisk). Feel free to choose any of the remainder that suit your needs.

A shopping list summarizing these items is in Appendix Two; the natural cleansing supplements are discussed in Chapter Ten.

**Juice extractor\*** You will need one of these to make fresh vegetable juices, but you don't have to invest in a top-of-the-range model and you can use it long after the detox is over. You can buy bottled vegetable juices, but making your own is far better because shop-bought varieties don't contain as many enzymes or as much life force as freshly made juices.

**Skin brush\*** This will be used for daily skin brushing, which is very helpful for both the lymphatic system and the skin. Make sure you get a brush made from natural bristle.

**Jug water filter\*** Tap water contains a lot of substances we don't really want in our bodies and a jug filter is the easiest way to remove some of these, especially heavy metals such as lead.

**Blender** Useful for making fruit smoothies in the summer and for blending homemade soups in the winter.

**Coffee grinder or food processor** For grinding flaxseeds, an important food during the detox. It's not essential to grind them, but grinding does enhance absorption.

**Food washing solution** You are encouraged to buy organic foods, but a washing solution will help remove any unwanted chemical or natural residues from fruits and vegetables. You can buy it in most health food stores.

**Tongue scraper** It's common to have a coated tongue during a detox and a tongue scraper will help deal with the problem. You can buy one from most dental practices and health food stores.

**Toothbrush** It's a good idea to start the detox with a new toothbrush, and to buy another one at the end. Your toothbrush collects a build-up of bacteria much quicker than you'd think, and ideally you should buy a new one at least once a month.

**Bicarbonate of soda/baking soda\*** This is a good addition to your usual oral hygiene routine, especially as it can help alleviate the problem of a coated tongue. You can also add it to your bath to help your body eliminate toxins through the skin. About 250g/½ pound per bath is the recommended amount, but don't use it more than twice a week as it can be slightly draining. Make sure the water is not too hot and soak for at least 15 minutes, then rest for at least an hour afterwards.

**Rebounder** A rebounder or mini-trampoline is excellent for improving the functioning of the lymphatic system, plus it's a lot of fun and good for aerobic fitness as well. You can be as gentle or as energetic as you like: I recommend starting with five minutes and gradually building up to fifteen.

**Skipping rope** Skipping is good for stimulating the lymphatic system, but not recommended if you have back problems or weak knees. Instead, choose a rebounder as this has a much gentler effect on the joints. Five to ten minutes a day of skipping in the fresh air is very invigorating.

**Body exfoliating cream** While you're doing lots of good things on the inside, there's no harm in doing a little bit of pampering on the outside as well. Exfoliating is a great way of removing dead skin cells. Doing it once a week will enhance the elimination abilities of the skin, and it will leave the skin feeling silky smooth and glowing.

## Introducing energy exercises

I've already mentioned the importance of energy and life force in food. In fact, every living thing is made of energy, including ourselves, and this has always been recognized in eastern philosophies (but pretty much ignored in the West until relatively recently). It's not merely an abstract concept – energy can be felt and seen – and many complementary therapies such as acupuncture, homeopathy, flower remedies, cranial-sacral therapy and energy healing are based on it. The fundamental principle is that changing a person's energetic flow will produce improvements in health and well-being.

In yoga, energy (or life force) is referred to as *prana*, and yogic breathing exercises are called *pranayama*. As anyone who has done yoga will know, practicing breathing exercises is a fantastic way of increasing your energy and life force – after a short period of doing these exercises you feel simultaneously invigorated and calm. The benefit is not just because you fill your body with more oxygen, it's also because you are filling yourself with more *prana* or energy. The Chinese have their own history of working with energy, they refer to life force/energy as *chi*, and specific exercises such as *tai chi* and *chi gung* have been developed over thousands of years to balance and enhance the energy field.

To give you a better picture of the value of energy and life force, here are some everyday examples:

- Contrast the difference between an apple that has just been picked from a tree with one that was picked two weeks ago – it's obvious that the freshly picked apple contains a much higher level of life force than the other one.
- Do you know someone who has such a positive aura about them that when they walk into a room everyone immediately becomes aware of their presence and feels lifted or inspired? This is a person who naturally has a high life force.
- Different places have different types of energies. Standing by a waterfall, walking through a rain forest or by the sea make you feel energized and invigorated because these are high-energy places. Visiting a derelict, run-down building can make you feel depleted because the place itself is depleted of energy.

Primarily based on yoga breathing practices and *chi gung*, the energy exercises on the detox programme are safe and simple methods for rebalancing and strengthening your energy field. They will get your energy moving and build up your vital life force, so that after a week or so of doing them you should have more energy, need less sleep, and feel generally more resistant to stress-provoking situations. The best way of grasping the concept of energy is for you to experience it yourself – turn to page 115 for a hand exercise that will show you this.

## Introducing lifestyle projects

These cover a wide range of different things you can try during the detox, including suggestions for the home and ideas for creating a pollution-free environment. There are also suggestions for activities that can enhance the detox, like lymphatic drainage massage that helps the detox process by moving and clearing lymph fluid. You are free to choose the ones that appeal to you.

## chapter 9

# Personalizing Your Programme

Each of us has a unique body-mind configuration with specific areas of resilience and vulnerability – a similar stressful experience can result in a headache or indigestion for some of us, high blood pressure for others. We also have individual tendencies towards specific complaints: some of us are prone to constipation, others to skin problems. By the same token, two people can eat the same food on a regular basis and while one will develop a food intolerance the other won't.

Our individual dispositions can affect the health of each of our elimination channels. For example, in some cases the digestive system may be overburdened while other channels such as the liver and lymph are functioning well, yet in other cases the liver may be the elimination channel under the most strain. Of course, the individual elements of our elimination systems function as a unified team and a difficulty with one area will eventually affect the whole system, so it is important to work with each of the channels simultaneously while doing a detox.

It is also important – and helpful – to identify which parts of your system require the most attention. By taking account of your personal requirements in this way, you will be able to create a detox programme tailor-made to your needs, and more effective for you than a 'one-size-fits-all' kind of plan.

The questionnaires in this chapter are designed to give useful pointers about the functioning of the individual components of your elimination system. They require simple 'yes' or 'no' answers, so completing them shouldn't take too much time. Afterwards, read the interpretation section at the end of the chapter to identify which areas require the most attention – then you can take steps to work with a specific channel during the detox. This will involve adding nutritional supplements, which are discussed in Chapter Ten.

## Your Stomach

*Part A*

1  I get heartburn at least a few times a month  **yes/no**
2  I take indigestion tablets quite often  **yes/no**
3  I get a lot of gas in my stomach and burp often  **yes/no**
4  I find it hard to digest protein foods or rich meals  **yes/no**
5  I find it hard to digest fried food  **yes/no**
6  I feel very full and bloated after eating a medium-sized meal  **yes/no**
7  My breath can smell bad even though I take proper dental care  **yes/no**
8  My sense of taste and smell is not as good it used to be  **yes/no**

*Part B*

1  I drink coffee and/or tea regularly  **yes/no**
2  I smoke or have smoked in the past  **yes/no**
3  I eat quickly  **yes/no**
4  I often skip meals and my eating pattern is irregular  **yes/no**
5  I am over forty  **yes/no**
6  I can lose my temper quite easily  **yes/no**
7  I tend to worry a lot  **yes/no**
8  There is a lot of stress in my life  **yes/no**

Score one point for each **'yes'**

**Total Score: Part A**

**Total Score: Part B**

## Your Intestines

1  I have a bowel movement at least once a day  **yes/no**
2  I have taken a course of antibiotics in the last year  **yes/no**
3  I have rarely had antibiotics in the past  **yes/no**
4  I am (or was) on the contraceptive pill  **yes/no**
5  I eat at least three portions of fruit and vegetables a day  **yes/no**
6  I get abdominal bloating regularly  **yes/no**
7  I drink 1½ litres/1½ quarts water daily  **yes/no**
8  I get diarrhoea a few times every month  **yes/no**
9  I don't need to strain when I have a bowel movement  **yes/no**
10  I get flatulence (wind) quite frequently  **yes/no**
11  I never use laxatives  **yes/no**
12  My stools are usually hard and in small segments  **yes/no**
13  I eat live (bio) yogurt at least twice a week  **yes/no**
14  My stools are runny  **yes/no**
15  I take steps to manage the stress in my life  **yes/no**
16  I have haemorrhoids  **yes/no**
17  I take regular exercise at least three times a week  **yes/no**
18  If I feel upset I tend to keep it bottled up inside  **yes/no**
19  I make sure I keep my alcohol intake low  **yes/no**
20  I drink at least two cups of coffee each day  **yes/no**
21  I try to avoid foods that contain refined sugar  **yes/no**
22  I like yeast-containing foods (e.g. Marmite, bread)  **yes/no**

**Score one point for each 'no' to an odd-numbered question**

**Score one point for each 'yes' to an even-numbered question**

**Total Score**

## Your Liver

1  I find it difficult to digest fatty foods  **yes/no**
2  I often feel tired for no apparent reason  **yes/no**
3  I have dark circles under my eyes  **yes/no**
4  I drink alcohol regularly  **yes/no**
5  I smoke cigarettes  **yes/no**
6  My stools are pale in colour  **yes/no**
7  The whites of my eyes are not as clear as they used to be  **yes/no**
8  My skin has a tendency to be spotty and/or greasy  **yes/no**
9  My stools float  **yes/no**
10  I eat a lot of high-protein foods (meat, cheese)  **yes/no**
11  I use (have used) recreational drugs  **yes/no**
12  Over the years I've had quite a lot of prescribed medication  **yes/no**
13  I don't exercise regularly  **yes/no**
14  I feel irritable quite often  **yes/no**

Score one point for each **'yes'**

**Total Score**

## Your Other Elimination Channels

1  I often have bladder irritation  **yes/no**
2  I am prone to urinary tract infections  **yes/no**
3  My urine is dark in colour  **yes/no**
4  My urine has a pungent smell  **yes/no**
5  I tend to get fluid retention  **yes/no**
6  I like to add table salt to my meals  **yes/no**
7  I eat quite a lot of protein foods (meat, dairy, fish, eggs)  **yes/no**
8  I like fatty foods  **yes/no**
9  I like sugary foods  **yes/no**
10  I don't take much physical exercise  **yes/no**
11  I don't sweat easily or I frequently use antiperspirant products  **yes/no**
12  I rarely have a sauna or massage  **yes/no**

Score one point for each **'yes'**

**Total Score**

**Your Combined Score**
Record your combined score here
(= sum of all the scores in this chapter)

## Interpreting your results

### 1 The stomach

The questions in this chart were designed to assess the functioning of your digestive enzymes, which are necessary to adequately digest and absorb food. Too many or too few enzymes can contribute to digestive problems: an excess can provoke ulcers, while a depletion increases the possibility of digestive complaints such as abdominal bloating, flatulence and leaky gut. Food intolerance can also be associated with a lack of digestive enzymes.

The questions in Part A are indicators that your enzymes may be depleted. Indigestion is usually interpreted as a sign of excess stomach acid, the solution for which is antacid tablets, but indigestion may equally indicate a lack of stomach enzymes and taking antacid tablets will only make the problem worse.

If you scored four or more for Part A, your digestive enzymes may be somewhat depleted and it may be useful to try some of the natural strategies for stimulating your enzyme production that are outlined in Chapter Ten. The foods that you are encouraged to eat during the detox are easy to digest, so they won't put extra strain on your enzyme system.

The questions in Part B are dietary, lifestyle and emotional factors that can disrupt and deplete digestive enzyme production. A score of four or more suggests you are taxing your digestive enzymes unnecessarily. You will benefit from reducing your risk factors in the long term by making some healthy dietary changes such as cutting down on coffee and eating regular meals.

### 2 The intestines

A perfect score of zero suggests that your digestive tract is functioning very well and that your diet and lifestyle choices are supporting the health of this system. A score of at least seven suggests your digestive system is functioning below par. A score of ten or more suggests that this part of your digestive system could definitely do with some support, so make sure you follow all the steps for supporting intestinal function in Chapter Ten.

It is very likely that you scored quite highly on this test if you have a food intolerance condition – as discussed in Chapters Four and Five food intolerance is usually associated with an imbalance of the digestive tract. The offending food often provokes digestive complaints such as constipation, diarrhoea or bloating, but once the food is removed from the diet these symptoms often subside.

During the detox you will be excluding the main culprit foods, which will give your digestive tract the opportunity to rebalance, but it is also important to take steps to strengthen this system if you want to avoid food intolerance in the future. This involves taking some natural nutritional supplements that can help to repopulate the colon with friendly bacteria, and other supplements that help to heal a leaky gut. In the unlikely event that you have food intolerance but scored less than ten on this test, you should still follow the recommendations for supporting the intestines given in Chapter Ten.

## 3 The liver

A score of seven or more suggests your liver may be overloaded and that your lifestyle choices are not supporting its proper functioning. Key indicators that suggest your liver may be struggling are questions 1, 6 and 9. Because the liver is so important as a detoxification organ, the Super Energy Detox includes specific nutritional supplements that assist the liver, and these should be taken by everyone. If you answered 'yes' to questions 1, 6 and 9, or your overall score was seven or above, then you may wish to follow the additional suggestions for working with the liver on page 66.

## 4 The other elimination channels

This chart focuses on the remaining channels – the kidneys, lymphatic system and skin. Bladder irritation or frequent urinary infections may suggest that your body's buffer systems are depleted (as discussed on page 40), so you should turn to Chapter Ten for the relevant steps to take. If your score is six or more the suggestions for working with the kidneys, lymph and skin should form part of your personalized detox programme.

## 5 The combined score

The body's elimination channels function as a unified team, so any problem with one channel will impair the other channels and eventually the overall system. This is why the detox programme is so effective, because it is designed to work with all the components of the team simultaneously. Completing the questionnaires should help you find out which channel or channels to focus on during the detox and you should get more from the programme by personalizing it in this way.

Now let's take a look at the combined score. As a guideline, any score above 25 suggests that your elimination system as a whole is not performing as well as it could and that you may very well be getting many symptoms you could do without.

## Re-doing the questionnaires

It can be worthwhile having another go at the questionnaires in this and previous chapters after you've completed the detox programme, because memories can be quite selective when it comes to health issues – we often forget that we used to suffer from a particular complaint on a regular basis. By retaking the questionnaires you will get a clearer indication of how your health has changed and it will also highlight any problem areas that require further attention.

Finally, transfer the scores from these questionnaires to the table on page 64. This will make it very easy for you to know which specific parts of the detox programme you need to follow.

## chapter 10

# The Cleansing Substances

These form a key part of the detox programme. The main foods and nutritional supplements should be taken by everyone, but if you have food intolerance there are specific recommendations for other substances you should take. The questionnaires in the previous chapter will help you personalize your programme so you can include extra substances to suit your individual needs, in addition to which there are two optional nutritional supplements you can include if they seem appropriate for you.

You should stop taking all of the cleansing substances at the end of the detox, unless otherwise indicated.

## 1 The main cleansing substances

These are the backbone of the programme, to be used by everyone. You will find a list of stockists at the end of this book, and instructions for taking them in Chapter Fifteen.

**Flaxseeds** (also known as linseeds) have a beneficial effect on the digestive system. They help to soothe and heal the lining of the intestines, plus they promote peristalsis, which assists with the cleansing process (but they don't have a laxative effect). Flaxseeds are also one of the best sources of omega-3 fatty acids, which support liver function and are good for the skin and the cardiovascular system.

Heat and light can easily damage flaxseeds, so they should be stored in a jar in the fridge. They are most easily absorbed as a powder, so grind them as you need them, or do a week's supply at the most.

**Psyllium** is derived from the husks of plantains (fruits similar to bananas), and is available as a powder or capsules. It provides bulk to the digestive tract, encouraging increased bowel movements that remove old waste matter from the digestive system. When psyllium is taken with a large glass of water, it swells up to form a jelly-like substance that has a soothing and cooling effect on the intestinal wall as it progresses through the digestive system. It helps to remove both excess mucus and impacted waste matter. Psyllium is not a laxative, but it will promote more frequent bowel movements, which is the whole idea. In fact, using psyllium has often been found to reduce the problem of diarrhoea or loose stools. It can also help to lower cholesterol.

**Milk thistle** (also called silymarin) is a herb that supports liver function. It's a powerful antioxidant that helps the liver in its important job of deactivating molecular compounds; it also helps the liver to rejuvenate and produce healthy new cells.

**MSM** stands for methylsulfonylmethane, available in powder or capsule form. Don't be put off by the name – all it contains is sulphur, a naturally occurring substance found in fruits, vegetables and sea plankton. MSM is included in the detox programme for its multiple benefits: it enhances detoxification and supports the liver; it supports the digestive tract and has a detoxifying effect on the body as a whole; it can improve the quality of the skin; it's helpful with joint aches and pains because of its anti-inflammatory effects; and it can also have a very mild laxative effect.

**A good multivitamin supplement** is a useful addition to the detox because it supplies antioxidants (vitamins A, C and E) and the whole spectrum of B vitamins. All of these nutrients are important for the body as a whole, but within the context of the detox they are a useful support for the liver and digestive system. Multivitamin supplements vary in quality: some brands use artificial ingredients rather than deriving vitamins from natural food sources, and some add unnecessary fillers or provide individual vitamins in an unbalanced ratio. See page 261 for information on good-quality supplements.

**Vitamin C** is a fantastic antioxidant and immune booster, vital for the liver to perform its detoxing activities adequately, and also good for the skin. A 1,000mg vitamin C supplement is included in the detox programme because of its beneficial support to the liver.

**A good multimineral supplement** will provide some important anti-oxidants such as zinc and selenium, and the alkaline-forming minerals calcium and magnesium. Mineral deficiency is extremely common, so it does no harm to invest in a good-quality multimineral supplement. The alkaline-forming minerals are needed by the body's buffer systems (page 40), which will be working hard while you are detoxing, and the minerals calcium, zinc and magnesium are essential to detoxify heavy metals such as lead, aluminium and cadmium.

There are many supplements that combine vitamins and minerals in one tablet, but it's preferable to take them separately – vitamins in the morning to give you energy, minerals before bed to help promote deep and restful sleep.

## The food intolerance programme

The main cleansing substances are extremely beneficial for food intolerance sufferers – flaxseeds and psyllium husks support the digestive tract, while MSM, milk thistle and vitamin C provide valuable support for the frequently overburdened liver. As intolerance is often associated with vitamin and mineral deficiencies, supplementation with these nutrients is also helpful.

Food intolerance and leaky gut (page 30) are frequently interlinked, so if you have food intolerance it is likely that you scored highly on the questionnaire for the intestines on page 56. However, even if your score was relatively low, it's still advisable to take the additional supports for the intestines (see page 65). Combined with the substances and supplements discussed above, this strategy will help strengthen your digestive tract, which is essential if you want to overcome your intolerance problem in the long term.

## Personalizing your programme

Quick Reference Guide

|  | Your Score | Use additional supports if score at least: |
| --- | --- | --- |
| The Stomach (Part A) |  | 4 |
| The Intestines* |  | 10 |
| The Liver |  | 7 |
| The Other Channels |  | 6 |

\* to be followed by food intolerance sufferers even if score is less than 10.

## Additional supports for the stomach

If your test results suggest that your digestive enzymes may be depleted, you can include either a natural digestive enzyme supplement *or* apple cider vinegar to your daily routine.

**Apple cider vinegar** stimulates the digestive juices and is particularly helpful for digesting protein, but don't use it if you suspect you have yeast sensitivity. Make sure you buy organic.

*Mix 1–2 teaspoons in a small amount of water and drink before lunch or dinner. It is not the most palatable of tastes, so an alternative option is to use a natural digestive enzyme.*

**Natural vegetarian digestive enzymes** are safe because they're totally derived from food sources such as papaya (pawpaw). Supplements that contain hydrochloric acid or animal extracts are to be avoided unless a nutritionist or doctor has recommended them for you.

*Take 1 capsule with larger meals (lunch and/or dinner), during or at the end of the meal. Don't take more than two a day.*

# Additional supports for the intestines

*To be taken by anyone who suspects they have food intolerance*

**FOS** stands for fructo-oligo-saccharides. It is a naturally occurring substance derived from vegetables such as cauliflower and asparagus that is used to provide 'food' for your friendly bacteria. Several studies have found that supplementing with FOS increases the level of friendly bacteria in your gut within a period of two weeks. It is available as capsules or powder, but the powder is more versatile because it can be sprinkled on food such as breakfast cereal, and it can even be added to hot drinks. Alternatively, you can just mix it with water.

Although FOS has a naturally sweet taste, it contains virtually no calories and is suitable for those with yeast sensitivity. It can produce flatulence in susceptible individuals, so if you get this reaction, simply stop taking it for a few days and then try it again at a reduced dose.

*Take 5–10g/1–2 teaspoons a day, at any time. It doesn't have to be stored in the fridge.*

**A good probiotic supplement** is simply a supplement of friendly bacteria that helps rebalance the eco-system of your gut. Get one that contains both the acidophilus and bifidus strains, and make sure that it is dairy-free. Keep it in the fridge, as the bacteria tend to die off at room temperature. You can buy it as powder or capsules – the capsules are normally absorbed better than the powder.

*Take 2 capsules or 1 teaspoon powder with a little water on an empty stomach each day. Before breakfast or last thing at night is ideal.*

**Glutamine** is an amino acid (protein) produced naturally by the body and used as a fuel by the digestive tract. When the digestive tract is not functioning up to par, glutamine levels in the body may be deficient, so taking a glutamine supplement can help improve things – it's highly beneficial for leaky gut in particular. Glutamine can also help with cravings for sugar, stimulants and alcohol, and it's beneficial for the lymphatic system, providing fuel for certain lymph cells. It is available as powder or capsules. The powder is particularly easy to take, as it is tasteless and mixes well with water.

*Take 2–4 grams glutamine powder a day (¼ teaspoon provides 1 gram), spreading the dose evenly (i.e. 2 grams in the morning and evening).*

## Additional supports for the liver

**Dandelion leaves** help clear congestion from the liver and stimulate bile production; they are also good for the kidneys and the digestive tract. You can get them in tincture or tablet form, but the easiest way of taking them is as a tea (dandelion coffee usually contains dairy extract and isn't suitable for the detox programme).

*Drink 1–2 cups of the tea each day.*

**Glutathione** is an amino acid (protein) made by the body from foods such as onions and garlic. It is a powerful antioxidant involved with several enzyme processes that support the liver. It is available in tablet form.

*Take 1 tablet a day, with food.*

## Additional supports for the other elimination channels

**Fresh parsley** is known to have a healing effect on the kidneys. It is quite potent, so should not be used in large quantities.

*A small amount of juiced parsley (about 1 handful) can be added to the daily detox juice drink every other day.*

**Cranberry extract** helps protect against urinary tract infections that can occur when you switch to an alkaline-forming diet if your buffer systems are depleted (see Chapter Seven). Cranberry juice generally doesn't have the active ingredient (due to processing) and it also contains either sugar or the sugar-substitute aspartame, both of which should be avoided.

You can buy the extract in powder or capsule form. The powder can be mixed with water or sprinkled on fruit or cereal.

*If you are prone to urinary tract problems, take 1 capsule (or ¼ teaspoon powder) cranberry extract a day, with food.*

**Dandelion leaves** have a gentle diuretic effect and help to reduce fluid retention.

*Drink 1–2 cups of the tea each day.*

## Optional extras

There are two other nutritional supplements that can be useful additions to your detox programme. Feel free to take them if they seem appropriate for you.

**Lecithin** is a rich source of choline and inositol, two B vitamins necessary for proper liver function, and it helps emulsify fats, making them easier to absorb; it can also help reduce cholesterol. If you have difficulty digesting fatty foods, or have a gall bladder or cholesterol problem, you may find lecithin beneficial. It is available in capsule or granule form. Granules are convenient as they can be sprinkled on cereal or fruit salad, mixed into yogurt, blended with juices or smoothies, or simply eaten straight. Lecithin is usually derived from soya, so it is not suitable if you have an intolerance to this food.

*Take 1 tablespoon lecithin granules a day, preferably with food (keep it in the fridge as it damages easily in heat and light).*

**Wheat grass** contains high levels of antioxidants and trace elements, is both highly alkalizing and strongly detoxifying, and particularly beneficial for the kidneys and lymph. It doesn't contain the wheat grain, so you can take it if you have wheat intolerance. Freshly squeezed wheat grass juice is best, and you can get it in some health food stores and restaurants where they have a special juice extractor to make it. Don't drink more than 50ml/¼ cup juice a day because its detoxifying effects are very powerful. In fact, the powdered version is much easier to take.

**Green food powders** are available that contain a mixture of wheat grass and other substances, such as chlorella, spirulina and green kamut. Choose whichever one appeals to you most (they tend to be quite expensive).

*Add 1 tablespoon wheat grass or other green food powder to water or the detox juice drink each day.*

## chapter 11

# Integrating the Programme into Your Daily Life

The Super Energy Detox shouldn't create too many extra demands on your time (activities such as skin brushing, juicing and energy exercises should require less than an hour a day), but preparation and planning are key to making it really simple to follow.

## Before you start

- Do a mini spring clean of your kitchen cupboards. Throw away any oils, nuts, dried fruits and packaged foods that have been sitting there for some time.
- Empty one cupboard for your own personal use during the detox. This keeps your things separate from the foods that others may be eating.
- Go on a shopping trip the week before so that you have all the equipment, nutritional supplements, oils, nuts, seeds and wheat-free and gluten-free grains and cereals you need.

## During the programme

- Buy fresh food twice a week and wash all the fruits and vegetables when you get home. It's then very quick and easy to prepare juices, salads and smoothies when you want them – just grab the ingredients from the fridge and off you go.

- The detox menu plan is designed to help you – you don't have to stick rigidly to it. Choose recipes you find appealing or devise your own according to the guidelines in Chapters Fourteen and Fifteen. Decide what you are going to eat for a few days in advance and then shop accordingly. This way you won't find yourself stuck, wondering what on earth to eat.

- It's unlikely you'll have a lot of spare time in the mornings, so organize things the night before to avoid having a mad rush when you get up. Before you go to bed, sort out the daily supplements for the following day (you can keep tablets in a used vitamin bottle or a pillbox).

- Unless there's a health food restaurant near your work, you will probably need to take your lunch with you. This really isn't difficult if you prepare what you need the night before and keep it in the fridge. When you get up in the morning, all you need to do is pack it and go.

- Keep plenty of snack food at work (or in your car or briefcase if you travel a lot), so you won't find you're hungry with nothing suitable to eat. Keep bottled water and herbal teas at work too.

- Activities such as juicing, skin brushing and energy exercises are recommended on a daily basis, and there are new energy exercises for you to experiment with each week. Familiarize yourself with the activities for the week and then plan how these will fit best into your daily routine. It's generally much easier (and less time-consuming) to get into the habit of doing new activities when they are scheduled into specific time slots.

- Don't become obsessive about things – you're supposed to be enjoying yourself, not adding extra stress to your life. Be flexible and relaxed. If something happens that interrupts your daily schedule, just slot the activities in later that day. To get the best out of the programme, it's important to try and complete all of the daily activities, but if you miss something out once in a while it won't be the end of the world.

## Time for yourself

The three-week programme has been designed to be gentle enough for you to continue with your usual daily activities such as work or looking after the children, but you should also try to allow plenty of time for yourself. Many people feel more introspective during a detox and they need time just to be still and reflect upon life. A hectic social schedule will take you out of this space, so avoid filling up your diary with too many social activities.

The detox is also a good opportunity to pamper yourself, so spend an evening giving yourself a facial and a manicure, or catch up with a good book or a video. Aim to spend time with people who understand what you're doing and who are supportive of you, avoiding anyone who might upset you.

## A detox journal

It can be useful to make a record of the changes you experience while you're following the detox. You don't need to do this on a daily basis (unless you feel like it), but it can be helpful to keep track of changes in your well-being. Here are a few examples of possible diary entries, which will also give you an idea of what to expect during the detox – there's more on this topic in the next chapter.

- Day 3: Feeling groggy. Would love a coffee and a piece of toast but I'm going to stick with the programme. The tiredness and cravings will probably pass soon.
- Day 5: Tummy bloating has disappeared, but still feel tired. Felt great after practising belly breathing. Must get into the habit of doing this regularly.
- Day 7: Woke up feeling very alert and awake, full of energy. Great. Haven't felt like this in ages. Wore my favourite jeans – they fitted perfectly.
- Day 9: Noticed I don't seem so tired when I get in from work. Haven't felt like that for months. Also, didn't feel so overwhelmed when we had a crisis at work. Generally feel much calmer and more balanced.

- Day 10: Had fairly loose stools today and I've got a slight headache. Two friends told me I'm looking really well. Made me feel good. My skin seems much clearer and my eyes look really bright.
- Day 15: I've got so much more energy and I need less sleep. Achieved a lot today and feel really positive about myself. Jane's coffee smelt awful – how on earth did I drink six cups of that stuff a day?

Journal writing is a very good way of working with your emotions. It can shed insight on your present life and where you would like it to head in the future. One of the best things that I like about going on a detox is the level of mental clarity I experience: my mind feels really sharp and clear and I can recall lots of 'lightbulb moments' about my life. This is another reason why it's useful to have plenty of private time to yourself during the detox – it can be really valuable to step off the treadmill of life to give yourself time to reflect on where your life journey is taking you.

Research has found that spending just 20 minutes writing about your feelings can have a positive impact on your immune system, because you are expressing your emotions rather than keeping them bottled up inside. The acid-forming stress hormones are being let go, allowing positive, health-promoting endorphins to be released.

## Exercise

If you don't normally exercise much, the detox is the perfect time to get more active because you're encouraged to take some light exercise such as walking, swimming and cycling every day. If you regularly do strenuous workouts at the gym, you may find you need to cut back on your exercise routine a bit, but this really depends on how you feel while you're doing the programme. If you feel great and energetic, then by all means continue with your usual routine, but if you feel a bit tired (this can happen in the early part of the programme), then don't force yourself. Aim to follow your natural body rhythms and you should be fine.

## chapter 12

# What to Expect

## Detox side effects

As your body starts to mobilize stored toxins and dispose of them via your elimination system, you may experience side effects such as headaches and tiredness. All detox programmes produce some side effects, but you can minimize their impact – in fact it's important to avoid side effects wherever possible. Releasing stored waste matter at too fast a rate puts a great deal of unnecessary strain on your body, and on an already overburdened elimination system in particular.

The key to reducing side effects is to detox at a slow and steady pace, and this will also make the detox more effective. It's a bit like spring cleaning – it wouldn't be very sensible to bring all your storage boxes up from the cellar to sort them out in one go because this would just create chaos. Far better to take a methodical approach and sort out a few boxes at a time. This way the job ultimately gets done faster and more effectively, without causing undue stress in the process.

The first week of the programme consists of a 'lightening the load' week. To continue with the house cleaning analogy, before you bring the boxes up from the cellar you need to make room for them by clearing away any clutter on the stairs and in the hall. In a similar fashion, the first week of the programme is preparing your body for deeper cleansing in the second and third weeks, and this should minimize any side effects.

If you scored highly on the Lifestyle Challenge (page 18), the first week of the detox will be very helpful because it will give your body breathing space to rebalance and strengthen before the deeper cleanse that follows in the second and third weeks.

Removing stimulants from your diet can also give you side effects, in addition to the ones you get from the detox. For example – it's extremely common to get withdrawal symptoms such as headaches and lethargy for a few days after removing coffee from your diet. It's better to deal with these during the first week before progressing to the deeper detox in the subsequent weeks. This is identical to clearing the clutter from your stairs and hall before bringing up the boxes from the cellar.

## Removing suspect intolerant foods

The first week of the detox also gives you the opportunity to remove any foods you think you may be intolerant of, and this can produce a variety of side effects in itself, including tiredness, headaches, digestive upset, feeling 'spaced out' and unable to concentrate. Don't worry – these symptoms generally pass within three to five days.

Not everyone experiences a negative reaction when they stop eating a culprit food, but if you do get minor symptoms, confining them to the first week of the programme gets them out of the way before you move on to the deeper cleansing of Weeks Two and Three. This is much kinder to the body than throwing it into deep cleansing while it's working hard dealing with the removal of intolerant foods.

## What to expect

The Super Energy Detox is designed to guide your body through the detox at a slow and steady pace, which should minimize side effects – you could sail through with none at all. Some changes to your bodily habits (such as more frequent bowel movements) are actively encouraged, because they're necessary to help mobilize and remove unwanted waste matter. Other side effects, such as headaches and tiredness, can hopefully be avoided, or at least reduced to a minimum. In fact, when waste products are eliminated efficiently (via the bowels, urine, breath and sweat), the chances of negative side effects are significantly less.

The following section will help you understand what particular side effects and symptoms may mean. It covers the common experiences people have when detoxing, explains why these symptoms can arise, and offers suggestions to minimize their effects. The fundamental principle you should follow is to listen to the messages coming from your body. Aim to follow your unique body rhythms and adapt the structure of the programme to meet your own particular needs.

## Tiredness, fatigue, headaches, brain fog

- You may feel tired or have a headache during the first week, especially if you've given up stimulants such as coffee. These are withdrawal symptoms that often occur when stimulants are removed from the diet. In fact, the tiredness may have been with you for a while, but it was masked by artificially pepping yourself up with stimulants. Follow your body's messages – if it wants to catch up on sleep, get some early nights.
- These symptoms can also occur when an intolerant food is removed from your diet. If you suspect this is the case, drink plenty of water and allow yourself time to rest. The withdrawal effects of removing an intolerant food usually pass within three to five days.
- If you get a headache, try the headache relief massage on page 112.
- You should find that your energy rebounds by the end of the first week.
- You may get the odd headache or short period of tiredness during the second and third weeks. This is a common detox experience related to waste products being mobilized and removed from the body. Drink plenty of water, take some light exercise (if you feel up to it), and rest when you feel you need to.

## Feeling a bit light-headed or 'spaced out'

- This can sometimes happen when a culprit food is removed from the diet. It should pass within two to three days (therefore, if it's related to intolerance it will occur in the first week only).
- It can also be a sign that your blood sugar has fallen too low. You are encouraged to eat three meals a day plus some snacks in between to avoid this happening. Try eating a light snack if you feel this way – the best thing to have is a complex carbohydrate food combined with

a little protein (eg. dairy-free yogurt with a banana and a sprinkling of pumpkin seeds, or hummus on rice cakes with a few raw vegetables).

- It can be a sign that your body is cleansing at too fast a rate. You can slow down the rate by following the eating guidelines given in the above point.
- After eating something, practise the grounding exercise on page 108.
- Make sure you relax until these feelings have passed. Avoid driving if you feel light headed.

## Digestive changes

- It's common – and beneficial – to experience some changes in bowel function. One of the principles of the detox is to gently remove old residues from the digestive tract, and this means that you should have more frequent bowel movements.
- Digestive function may alter when an intolerant food is no longer eaten, and many people get constipation for a couple of days. Try to avoid using laxatives, take an extra gram (1,000mg) of vitamin C instead.
- The detox diet contains a large amount of natural fibre and you will also be adding extra fibre in the form of psyllium from Week Two onwards, so after your bowels have stabilized you should have more frequent bowel movements. You may find that you are having 2–3 bowel movements a day rather than one.
- It's also quite normal to have loose stools for a few days while your digestive system adjusts to the new diet.
- The detox juice drink that you will be taking from Week Two onwards has a powerful detoxifying effect. It stimulates peristalsis so you may need to go to the loo soon after drinking it, and for some people it causes loose stools. If this is the case for you, stop the drink for a few days and then try it again.
- The beetroot (beet) in the detox drink will change the colour of your stools.
- You may have diarrhoea a couple of times during the programme (diarrhoea means very watery stools as opposed to loose stools or more frequent bowel movements). If you get diarrhoea more often, cut out the psyllium, intestinal supplements, MSM and detox drink. If the symptom stabilizes, add the supplements back at a reduced level (half

the recommended amount). If you get frequent diarrhoea it's unlikely to be caused by the detox, so check with your doctor if this symptom persists.

## Urinary changes

- Taking a multivitamin supplement will make your urine more yellow – this is due to the effect of one of the B vitamins and is completely harmless.
- You are encouraged to drink lots of water, so you will need to make more frequent trips to the loo.
- Fluid retention often shifts during an alkaline-forming detox diet. Again, this will mean you need to pee more often as the excess fluid is removed.
- Removing an intolerant food from the diet can also shift excess fluid.
- If you are prone to bladder infections, take a cranberry extract supplement to reduce this risk (more information on this on page 66).

## Your weight

- The Super Energy Detox is NOT a weight loss programme.
- There are no restrictions on the quantity of food you can eat – you can eat as much as you want. In fact, you are encouraged to eat three meals a day and snacks in between.
- You won't be having the empty calories found in things like cookies, crisps, chocolate, chips and alcohol, so this will have a beneficial impact if you are trying to lose weight.
- It's possible for weight to be lost when an intolerant food is removed from the diet (a food intolerance condition can sometimes make it difficult to lose weight even when a calorie-controlled diet is followed). For more information on this subject, read our book *Lose Wheat Lose Weight,* also published by Thorsons.
- Shifting excess fluid will result in weight loss, but this is different from losing adipose tissue (fat).

## Your emotions

In Chapter Two I discussed how a detox programme often helps establish a better connection with your body's communication system – after removing the load that the elimination system has to process, it's easier to recognize the messages coming from the body. It is via the body that we feel our emotions, so by the end of the programme we should also have a clearer connection to our emotions. As the body, mind and emotions effectively function as a unified team, any changes we make on a physical level are likely to have an impact on our emotions and minds as well. While we are cleansing the physical body, we can also experience an 'emotional detox', meaning that old emotions we previously ignored come to the surface to be released. Not everybody experiences this, but if you do, the following points may be helpful.

- You may experience only positive changes to your emotions. This is fine.
- You may notice that your emotions are a bit up and down. This is fine too. The best thing to do with emotions is to let them flow in a healthy fashion.
- Use this increased contact with your emotions to get to know yourself on a deeper level. Ask yourself why you are feeling a particular emotion and what it is trying to tell you about your life.
- Remember that not every emotion is worthy of in-depth analysis. Feeling irritable could just be a signal that your blood sugar has fallen too low rather than telling you something of major significance about your life.
- Detoxing can sometimes bring old emotions to the surface. You may find yourself thinking about someone who was close to you but who is no longer in your life and this may make you feel weepy. Let the emotion express itself by having a bit of a cry. Afterwards you will probably notice that you feel lighter, clearer and 'cleansed' of the emotion.
- If you do have a major 'light bulb moment', it's best not to be too hasty about making any major decisions about your life. Write down your feelings and insights in your journal, wait for the end of the detox and then review it.

## Other changes

- Your tongue may become coated. This is a normal symptom when following a detox. A tongue scraper will remove the coating and gargling with a solution of bicarbonate of soda/baking soda is also highly effective (*2 teaspoons mixed with a little water*).
- You may notice that your body odour becomes stronger. This is normal; it signals that the body is clearing wastes through your skin. You will probably need to have more frequent baths and showers during the programme.
- It is also possible to have bad breath or have a bad taste in your mouth. Brushing your teeth frequently and/or using a mouthwash can help.

## The good stuff

- This chapter has focused on detox side effects, but don't lose sight of why you are doing a detox. It's not all doom and gloom, and the benefits usually start to manifest themselves pretty quickly – generally by the middle of Week Two if not before.
- By the end of the three-week programme you should notice lots of positive changes to your well-being.

## chapter 13

# The Summer
# and Winter Eating Plans

You can do the Super Energy Detox at any time of year, there's even a choice of eating plans for summer and winter.

## Eating with the seasons

Everything in life follows a cycle – tides ebb and flow, day turns into night, and the planets rotate in a specific sequence around the sun. The body too has its own rhythms and cycles: there is the 24-hour circadian cycle that governs the body's internal clock so we feel alert during the day and sleepy at bedtime; there is the monthly hormonal cycle that governs female reproduction and menstruation; and there are the longer-term cycles that govern major life transitions such as puberty and menopause.

The natural rhythms of the seasons affect us in subtle yet powerful ways, influencing our mood and energy levels. In summer we are more likely to feel outgoing and energized, enjoy physical pursuits and sport and choose active holidays. In winter we usually feel more introspective and prefer activities that are relaxing, and we often need more sleep than in the summer months.

## Raw foods

Raw foods are most beneficial to our health because they contain high levels of vitamins and enzymes. They're excellent energy foods as their life force is extremely high, whereas foods that have been overcooked are depleted of their nutrient content and life force. For this reason, many natural health practitioners advocate a diet that is high in raw foods throughout the year, but I believe this can have a debilitating effect because our digestive systems are also influenced by the seasons.

Your digestive 'fire' is at its strongest during the warm summer months and at its weakest when the weather is cold. Despite being high in nutrients, raw foods have a cooling effect on the body and the digestive system finds it difficult to assimilate them when your digestive fire is low in the winter. Too many raw foods in winter can cause indigestion, bloating, flatulence and frequent peeing. They can also deplete your vital life force, sap your energy and make you feel excessively tired.

Not everybody experiences ill effects from eating raw foods in winter – some people can tolerate them because they have a naturally strong digestive fire. You are most likely to be negatively affected if you have a tendency to gain weight easily, frequently suffer with indigestion and bloating, need lots of sleep and have a pale complexion.

The summer eating plan focuses on deriving maximum benefits from the huge variety of fresh raw foods available during this season. Fresh fruits, salads and smoothies are the major players in the detox at this time, while the winter eating plan consists of foods such as stir-fries, roasted vegetables and nourishing hot soups that have a heating and warming effect on the body. (Light cooking such as stir-frying doesn't significantly affect the nutritional value and life force potential of these foods.)

Certain foods have natural healing and cleansing properties that make them extremely valuable in the detox programme and wherever possible they have been included in the menu plans.

## Summer foods

### Papaya (pawpaw) and pineapple

Both of these fruits contain natural enzymes (papain in papaya and bromelain in pineapple) that help the digestive system. Papaya is also a good source of the antioxidant beta-carotene, which can help heal the digestive tract. If you think your digestive enzymes may be depleted, try to have a small portion of either of these fruits *before* eating a large meal, especially one that contains protein. (As a general rule, only eat fruit before a meal or at least two hours after finishing a large meal.) If you don't particularly like the taste of these fruits, disguise them by blending them with some other fruits into a smoothie.

### Berries, black cherries and red grapes

These fruits, but especially blueberries, are fantastic as part of your detox diet. They are a very rich source of a potent group of antioxidants called anthocyanidins that have an even greater protective effect on the body than vitamin E. They are excellent foods for the liver because they work in conjunction with the liver support formulations you will be taking (e.g. MSM), making them much more effective. These fruits also have a healing effect on the digestive system, helping to heal a leaky gut, and they are also high in vitamin C. Blueberries are great blended into a smoothie (mixed with watermelon and strawberries they're particularly delicious), while cherries and red grapes make a great snack in between meals, and are really good in fresh fruit salads. Try to eat lots of these fruits through-out the summer months, even after you've finished the detox.

### Sprouting seeds

These are a high life-force food. They provide an easily digestible and fat-free source of protein and are very alkaline-forming; they also con-tain enzymes that support the function of the digestive system. Look in your health food store for alfalfa and the bags of mixed sprouts (which usually contain sprouted mung beans, chickpeas and lentils) and add a handful of each to your salad every day. They will keep fresh in the fridge for three to four days.

If you are feeling more adventurous and have the time, you can make your own sprouts. To make alfalfa, take a small handful of the seeds and soak them in a small amount of water for about eight hours. Throw the soaking water away, rinse the seeds and put them in a jar in a cool, dark place (a kitchen cupboard is ideal). Rinse the growing seeds in fresh water twice a day – they will be ready to eat in about five days.

## Winter foods

### Ginger

Root ginger has been used as a digestive tonic in China and India for thousands of years. It has a healing and warming effect on the digestive system and acts as a gentle digestive enzyme, so it can be helpful for all types of digestive complaints. It also has anti-inflammatory properties and is well worth including in your detox if you suffer with joint aches and pains; it is also known to improve circulation.

Use fresh root ginger chopped or sliced in stir-fried vegetables or to flavour soups. One of the easiest ways of making it a regular part of your daily diet is to make ginger tea. Chop up about 2½ cm/1 in of the root and bring to the boil in a pan of water. Simmer for 5 minutes, strain and sweeten with honey to taste.

### Onions, garlic and leeks

These vegetables are included in the detox because they have a beneficial effect on the digestive system. All three (but especially garlic) have antibacterial and antifungal properties, useful for correcting an imbalance in the flora residing in the gut, and particularly good if you are suffering with food intolerance or suspect that you have yeast sensitivity. Foods in the onion family are also naturally rich in sulphur that, like MSM, is beneficial for the liver's detoxification activities.

### Cruciferous vegetables

These are the brassica family (cabbage, broccoli, kale, Brussels sprouts and cauliflower), which offers numerous benefits to health. All contain FOS (page 65) that acts as nourishment for the friendly bacteria in the gut; they also contain lots of healthy soluble fibre.

The cruciferous vegetables also play a useful role in balancing female hormones, which can be helpful in cases of pre-menstrual tension, fibroids and endometriosis; scientific research has also found that women who regularly eat these vegetables have a lower risk of developing breast cancer. Cabbage has many healing properties for the digestive system, but especially for the intestines and leaky gut. Broccoli is a true 'superfood' – as well as providing FOS, it is an extremely good source of antioxidant nutrients and minerals.

## chapter 14

# Super Energy Detox Week One

## Things to do this week

### Diet

- Have freshly squeezed lemon juice with water when you get up.
- Add 1 tablespoon ground flaxseeds to your breakfast cereal or juice every day.
- Drink 1 glass of freshly prepared carrot juice every day.
- Drink at least 1½ litres/1½ quarts water (filtered or mineral, not carbonated) every day.
- Follow all the eating guidelines in this chapter.

### Supplements

- Take a good-quality multivitamin tablet with your breakfast.
- Take a good-quality multimineral tablet before going to bed.

### Personalized programme

- If you are following recommendations for the stomach, start taking either apple cider vinegar or a digestive enzyme now.
- If you are following the recommendations for the intestines, start taking the probiotic supplement, FOS and glutamine now.

*Refer back to Chapter Ten for guidelines on how to take these supplements.*

## Energy exercises

• Spend 10–15 minutes every day practising belly breathing.

## Lifestyle projects

• Skin brush for 5 minutes every day.
• Take at least 15 minutes light exercise every day.
• Follow the guidelines for decluttering your home (optional).
• Start your journal (optional).

## Other things in this chapter

• Guidelines if you are yeast sensitive.

# The food intolerance programme

This programme excludes all the main food intolerance culprits – the gluten grains (wheat, oats, barley, rye), dairy products (milk, cheese, butter, yogurt), citrus fruits (except lemon which usually doesn't provoke reactions), sugar, yeast and alcohol. You should eliminate these foods from the first day of the programme and avoid them throughout the three-week period (they're not appropriate during a detox anyway, because of their acid-forming nature and low-nutrient value).

Other foods that have been found to provoke intolerance – such as eggs, soya produce and the nightshade family (potatoes, tomatoes, peppers and aubergines/eggplants) – are included in the programme, but if you know or suspect that you have an intolerance to any of these foods, simply omit them. If you know you are intolerant to any other food that is included in the programme, avoid this as well.

## Lightening your load

This first week of the detox is called 'lightening your load' week. The main purpose of this is to prepare your body for the deeper cleanse that you will be doing in the following two weeks. All the foods you need to avoid throughout the three-week programme will be removed from the first day of this week, and they are listed in the following chart. A full list of the foods allowed on the programme is in Appendix Four.

| Avoid | Substitute |
| --- | --- |
| *Food* | |
| Wheat-containing foods; eg. bread, cakes, biscuits, cookies, most breakfast cereals. The other gluten grains: oats, barley, rye | Rice cakes, non-gluten flours, gluten-free cereal grains, rice, quinoa, millet, buckwheat, millet flakes, buckwheat flakes |
| Cow's milk | Rice milk, nut milk, soya milk |
| Cheese, yogurt | Goat's milk/cheese/yogurt |
| | Soya milk/yogurt |
| | Sheep's milk/cheese/yogurt |
| Refined sugar | Honey (in very small amounts) |
| All meat | Fish (chicken in Week One only) |
| Eggs (except in Week One) | |
| Oranges, grapefruit | All other fresh fruits |
| Rhubarb | All other fresh fruits |
| Bananas (except in Week One) | All other fresh fruits |
| Peanuts | All other nuts |
| Dried fruits | Fresh fruits |
| Shellfish | Any other fish (Week One only) |
| Hydrogenated fats (vegetable spreads) | Cold pressed oils (olive, sunflower) |
| Processed and refined foods (including foods such as quorn) | Fresh, organic produce |
| Fried foods (except stir-fries) | Baked, steamed and grilled foods |
| Barbecued and burnt food | Baked, steamed and grilled foods |
| Salt | |

*Drinks*

| | |
|---|---|
| Coffee (including decaffeinated) | Dandelion tea, |
| Black tea (including decaffeinated) | ginger tea, all herb teas |
| Hot chocolate | |
| Malted drinks | Lemon water |
| Carbonated water | Vegetable juice (freshly prepared) |
| Alcohol | Water (mineral or filtered) |
| Cola and fizzy drinks | Fruit smoothies |
| Commercially prepared fruit juices | |
| Commercially prepared vegetable juices | |

*Other*
Cigarettes
Recreational drugs

## Food and drink to include this week

*(The bullet points in bold type are recommendations that you should aim to follow; the others are optional suggestions.)*

**Fruits** are important during the entire programme because they contain high levels of dietary fibre, antioxidant nutrients and life force, and nearly all types are alkaline-forming. If you are doing the detox in the winter, don't keep fruits in the fridge because this will have too strong a cooling effect. In fact, you may prefer to stew fruits lightly and eat them hot. Simply chop them roughly and heat them through in a pan with 2 tablespoons water for 2 minutes.

All fruits are allowed on the programme except oranges, rhubarb and bananas. Oranges can be associated with food intolerance; rhubarb is high in oxalic acid, which puts a strain on the kidneys. Bananas can have a sluggish effect on the digestive system and will slow down the cleansing process, but you can eat them in moderation in Week One if you find it hard doing without them at the start of the detox.

- **Have at least two pieces of fruit each day this week.**
- You can have a banana every other day this week, but avoid bananas altogether during the following two weeks.

**Vegetables** are highly important for the detox, as they are alkaline-forming and high in nutrient value, fibre and life force. All fresh vegetables are allowed throughout the programme. For your lunch and dinner during the summer, have a large mixed salad (including a handful of sprouting seeds) with some protein or grains, and don't forget that you can always nibble on raw vegetables between meals if you feel peckish. During the winter months, have steamed, baked or stir-fried vegetables with both your lunch and dinner.

• **Have at least two large portions of vegetables a day this week.**

**Grains** provide energy and essential nutrients such as B vitamins, so it's important to have a good quantity of high-quality grains in the detox. Brown rice is an excellent food because it has a natural cleansing effect on the elimination system, and even during the summer months you can add it (cooked and cooled) to salads. Experiment with other grains such as buckwheat, millet and quinoa, which can be cooked on their own or mixed with brown rice (quinoa is an excellent source of protein). Wheat-free and gluten-free cereals are widely available in flake form – look in your health food store for buckwheat, millet, brown rice and quinoa flakes, and feel free to make up your own mix. Serve with rice milk, goat's milk or soya milk.

• **Have one portion of brown rice at least every other day.**
• **Alternate this with one portion of any of the other grains with your main meals (lunch and dinner).**
• Flaked grains are excellent for breakfast.

**Pulses (legumes)** are a good source of complex carbohydrates that provide energy and essential nutrients, but they are acid-forming and tend to slow down the cleansing process, so it's best to keep these foods to a minimum.

• During this first week you can have a small portion of pulses (legumes), such as chickpeas (including hummus), kidney beans or lentils every day.

**Fish** provides easily digestible protein and essential fats – salmon, trout, tuna, sardines, haddock, halibut, cod, plaice, herring, mackerel, sea bass and sole are all good sources of these nutrients. Shellfish (eg. crab, lobster and prawns) is good because it is high in zinc, but it is also highly

acid-forming, so it is best avoided throughout the detox programme.
- During this first week you can eat three portions of fish.

**Meat** is not a good food during the detox programme, because it is both acid-forming and very difficult for the elimination system to process, but if you usually eat a lot of meat you may have a small portion of fresh chicken three times during this first week, to ease you into the programme gently. Try to buy organic, and have less than three portions if possible, then exclude all meat and poultry during Weeks Two and Three.

**Vegetarian protein** is much gentler for the elimination system to process than meat or fish protein, so if you are used to eating lots of meat and fish, this is a good opportunity to experiment with alternatives such as quinoa and tofu (bean curd). Quinoa has more protein weight-for-weight than steak, but without any of the saturated fat, antibiotics and hormones often added to meat, and it only takes 10 minutes to cook (even less time than rice). Tofu (bean curd) is great in stir-fries. Dairy-free live yogurt is another good source of protein and it helps the colon to repopulate with friendly bacteria. Eggs are allowed during this first week, but not in the following weeks.
- **Have one portion of dairy-free live yogurt every day.**
- **Have one other portion of protein food (fish, tofu, chicken) every day.**
- You can have up to three eggs this week.

**Nuts and seeds** are packed with nutrients and are a good source of both carbohydrates and protein. Almonds, Brazil nuts, hazelnuts, pecans and walnuts are all allowed, but not peanuts. Pumpkin and sunflower seeds make ideal snacks in between meals, and sesame seeds are good sprinkled on cereals and salads. All the nuts and seeds you eat should be fresh and unsalted.
- **Have one handful of mixed nuts and seeds every day.**
- You can have an extra handful if you like.

**Healthy dietary fat** is important during a detox programme. You will be getting essential fats from oily fish, nuts and seeds, but you may also have a small quantity of cold pressed oil. It can be used as a dressing (with lemon juice) on salads, instead of butter on baked potatoes, or to stir-fry vegetables (only use olive oil for stir-frying).

- You can have 1–2 tablespoons oil a day.

## How much to eat

Summer and winter eating plans are provided for Weeks Two and Three of the programme. During Week One you are free to choose any of the other recipes in the book that appeal to you. Throughout the detox you should plan to have three meals a day and a couple of snacks in between – it's a good rule to eat whenever you feel peckish so your blood sugar balance remains stable. You're not following a weight loss regime, so you don't need to limit your portion sizes.

The key foods to eat during this first week are lots of fruits and vegetables with moderate amounts of grains and smaller quantities of protein and fats. By doing this and avoiding acid-forming sugar, alcohol, gluten grains and dairy products, your diet will become more alkaline-forming.

### Morning lemon juice

- Your body's elimination system (especially your liver and digestive tract) is at its most efficient during the earlier part of the day, and freshly squeezed lemon juice first thing in the morning is a great way of spurring it into action.
- **Squeeze the juice of one medium-sized lemon and mix it with some water and a teaspoon of honey.**
- In the winter, make it with hot water and add a few pieces of fresh ginger.
- If you like the taste, you can have as many of these drinks as you like during the day.

## Make friends with your juicer

This first week is an opportunity for you to get to know your juicer. It's an extremely versatile piece of equipment and you should never get bored with juicing because there are so many wonderful combinations to concoct. One of the easiest, tastiest and most nutritious juices is carrot (to make one large glass of juice, you need about 500g/1lb carrots). Carrot juice is high in beta-carotene, a nutrient that supports the mucous membranes in the digestive tract and the lungs; it's also highly alkaline-forming and has immune-boosting properties.

Soft fruits are better suited to making smoothies, but some fruits are suitable for the juice extractor. Apples are great for juicing and are good with carrots (⅔ carrot to ⅓ apple). Pineapple flesh (without the skin) can also be juiced and once you've tried it freshly squeezed, you'll probably never want the shop-bought version again.

- **Have one large glass of carrot juice each day, or try carrot and apple, or carrot and celery.**
- You can have it at any time of day, but you should drink the juice as soon as it is made because the nutrient and enzyme content declines very quickly.
- Next week, you will be adding the detox juice drink to your programme.

## Water

Throughout the programme you need to drink a minimum of 1½ litres/1½ quarts filtered or bottled still water a day (don't have carbonated water because it creates a lot of gas in the digestive tract). This is an important part of the programme, as the water is needed to help flush old waste products through your system. If you're not in the habit of drinking this much water, it can be helpful to set up some type of 'drinking schedule' at regular intervals throughout the day.

- **Drink one large glass of water at 11am, 2pm, 4pm, when you get in from work, and finally at 9pm. This will provide the minimum recommended daily amount.**
- Don't drink too much water late in the evening or you may need to get up in the night to pee.
- Try not to drink too much water with main meals (lunch and dinner), because it dilutes the digestive enzymes. Either drink nothing at all, or just a small glass of water.
- Wait for about an hour after eating a large meal before drinking water again.

- With smaller meals (breakfast, snacks and fruit), it is fine to drink fluid.

## Adding flaxseeds to your diet

Flaxseeds are a valuable part of the programme because they have a beneficial effect on the digestive system. They don't have a very strong taste, so they can easily be added to food or drinks. You can eat the seeds as they are, or grind them first. Keep the seeds in an airtight container in the fridge (away from heat and light which make them go rancid), and don't grind up more than a week's supply at a time.

- **Have one tablespoon ground flaxseeds every day. The easiest way of taking them is to sprinkle them on your breakfast or mix them into your carrot juice.**
- If the seeds are not ground, mix 1–2 teaspoons into your breakfast.
- If you have time, you can soak the seeds overnight in a little water (just enough to cover them), then add the seeds and their soaking water to your breakfast in the morning. Soaking helps increase absorption.

## Energy exercise: belly breathing

How you breathe has a significant impact on your energy levels and how you feel. It's common to breathe shallowly from only the top portion of the lungs, but this shallow breathing depletes your energy levels, reduces your thinking capabilities and makes it more likely that you will experience stress.

In contrast to this, full breathing offers numerous health benefits: if you want to feel more energized, be able to achieve more with your time, handle stress better, feel calm and centred most of the time, then learn how to belly breathe.

This form of breathing also helps your body to detoxify – it helps remove toxins via the lungs and it also supports the movement of lymphatic fluid – and helps to tone and strengthen the digestive system.

The key to breathing correctly is to make sure your diaphragm muscle is moving with each breath. This muscle is located just under the rib cage and you will feel it clearly when you practise the guided sequence below. Set aside a 10–15 minute time slot when you won't be disturbed, and make sure your clothing is loose and comfortable, especially around the waist area.

- Lie on the floor. Place both feet about 18cm/6in away from your buttocks with your knees pointing straight up towards the ceiling. This position is great for your spine because your middle back is resting solidly against the floor. (If you don't find it comfortable, just lie completely flat on the floor with your legs straight.)
- Place one hand on your chest and the other on your stomach, just under your ribs (this is where your diaphragm muscle is).
- Breathe normally for about a minute and just observe the movement of the breath through your hands. Notice how and where the breath is flowing through your body.
- Breathing only through your nose, on your next inhale guide the breath down into your stomach (just focusing your mind on what you want to achieve will make this happen). The hand that is placed on your diaphragm muscle should rise. Once your belly has expanded as far as it can, continue inhaling into the top part of the lungs so the hand on your chest also rises.
- Exhalation reverses this sequence: first your chest will fall, then your belly.
- The inhale and exhale should be of equal lengths, so once you're feeling comfortable with the basic sequence, start counting (in your mind) along with the breath. Try to get the in-breath and out-breath to consist of eight slow counts each. Don't strain – follow a rhythm that you find comfortable. There should be no gap between the inhale and the exhale. Continue counting with the breath and observing your hands rising and falling for 3–4 minutes.
- The air we breathe contains energy and life force. Bring your attention to this fact and focus on the life force that is filling your body as you inhale. You may feel or visualize this as golden molecules of light and energy that fill your lungs and then proceed to fill every cell of your body, right from the top of your head to the bottom of your toes. Feel this energy revitalizing and healing your whole body. As you exhale, you may like to visualize any stress or tension leaving your body with the breath.

- Continue breathing and focusing on the life force in the breath for about five minutes.
- Some people can feel light-headed when they first try this exercise, so if this happens, just stop and breathe normally again. Remain on the floor and rest. The feeling will pass quickly. You shouldn't feel light-headed if you make sure that you go at your own pace – there's no need to force or strain.
- It's easiest to feel the rise and fall of your belly when you are lying on the floor, but when you've practised this exercise a couple of times try it in a sitting position (either cross-legged on the floor or sitting on a chair), keeping your spine straight and your body relaxed. When you feel comfortable with the routine in a sitting position you can practise it anywhere.

## Skin brushing

Skin brushing is extremely popular and for good reason – it's excellent for moving lymph fluid and for improving the quality of your skin. The best time to do it is first thing in the morning so that afterwards you feel really invigorated and ready to seize the day.

Skin brush on dry skin before your morning shower or bath and always brush in a direction towards the heart. Start with the feet and move up each leg using reasonably firm, upward strokes, then spend extra time on the tops of the thighs and buttocks (skin brushing is great for shifting cellulite). Be gentler on the stomach area and avoid the breasts completely. Brush up each arm and the areas of the back that you can reach comfortably. It only takes about five minutes to brush your whole body and it will leave you feeling invigorated and your skin fresh and tingling.

## Exercise

To help keep your elimination system working effectively, get at least 15 minutes light exercise every day during this first week. If you don't have a regular workout routine, one of the easiest ways of increasing the amount of exercise you take is by walking. Summer is the ideal time to go for long walks in the evening; in winter, wrap up warm and go for a brisk walk after supper. Think about ways in which you can avoid using the car or public transport and walk instead, or go for a swim or a gentle cycle ride.

It's definitely not a good idea to embark on a strenuous new fitness schedule while you're doing the detox as this will put too much strain on your body. Instead, build up your fitness levels gradually over the next three weeks with gentle activities, then you can take up a more serious exercise routine at the end of the programme if you like.

## Decluttering your home (optional)

While you're cleansing your physical body it's also a good idea to spend a little time on your home. Your physical energy can become depleted if you're spending time in an environment that you find displeasing and this will be affecting you subconsciously, even though you may not be aware of it on a conscious level.

Your home accumulates the energy of the emotions and feelings that are expressed there, and this also applies to the things that are in it. This is why we sometimes instinctively want to rearrange the furniture or do a good spring clean whenever we go through an important life change, such as starting a new relationship or job. Conversely, holding on to things that you no longer need or being surrounded by lots of clutter can have a depleting effect on your energy levels.

A good way of preparing yourself for the deeper cleansing of the physical body that you will be doing from next week is to spend a little time sorting out and organizing the things in your home. Before I start a large project, I always spend a day or so sorting out my office, and when I've done this, I find my mind is much clearer and my creative energy starts to flow.

This detox is mainly about looking after yourself, so it's not necessary to get out the mops and buckets and engage in a full spring clean (unless you really feel like it), but it is a good idea to spend a bit of time sorting out things like your clothes, make-up, piles of newspapers, magazines and paperwork, etc. You will probably feel physically lighter and mentally clearer after this has been done.

## If you are yeast sensitive

Many of the foods that provoke yeast sensitivity, such as sugar, alcohol and bread, are already excluded from the programme, but if you suspect that you have a yeast sensitivity (from the questionnaire on page 25) there are a few other things you need to do.

- Don't eat mushrooms or use vinegar.
- Avoid honey (FOS powder has a slightly sweet taste so this can be used as a substitute).
- Keep your fruit intake to a maximum of two pieces a day. One piece is equivalent to one slice of fresh pineapple, half a papaya (pawpaw), one apple or one peach. Eat more vegetables to make up for the reduced fruit component of the diet.
- Never eat fruits, nuts or seeds that have any signs of mould on them. Mould can grow if the food has been sitting on the supermarket shelf for a while – it shows as a white or brown 'fur' on foods.
- You can still use your juicer, but instead of one large glass of juice a day, drink two small glasses at different times. This applies particularly to carrot juice, so dilute it with water or make a juice with carrots and celery (50:50) instead.

## Planning your daily routine

To make the programme as easy as possible for you, I've devised a table to help you structure each of the daily detox activities into your normal routine. There is space at the bottom for you to write in the additional cleansing substances and supplements that form part of your personalized programme (the lifestyle projects are not included because they're optional activities). Similar tables are provided for Weeks Two and Three. You can photocopy them and stick them on the fridge.

| DAILY DETOX ACTIVITIES | | | | | | | |
|---|---|---|---|---|---|---|---|
| **Week One** | Day 1 | Day 2 | Day 3 | Day 4 | Day 5 | Day 6 | Day 7 |
| *Skin brushing* | | | | | | | |
| *Lemon juice* | | | | | | | |
| *Flaxseeds* | | | | | | | |
| *Multivitamin* | | | | | | | |
| *Multimineral* | | | | | | | |
| *Carrot juice* | | | | | | | |
| *Water* | | | | | | | |
| *Exercise* | | | | | | | |
| *Belly breathing* | | | | | | | |
| *Personal:* | | | | | | | |
| | | | | | | | |
| | | | | | | | |
| | | | | | | | |
| | | | | | | | |
| | | | | | | | |

## chapter 15

# Super Energy Detox Week Two

## Things to do this week

### Diet

- Continue with the freshly squeezed lemon juice and water when you get up.
- Continue adding 1 tablespoon ground flaxseeds to your breakfast cereal or juice.
- Drink 1 glass of the detox drink (page 101) instead of carrot juice every day.
- Continue with 1½ litres/1½ quarts water (filtered or mineral) every day.
- Follow all the eating guidelines given in this chapter.

### Supplements and cleansing substances

- Continue with the multivitamin tablet with breakfast.
- Continue with the multimineral tablet before bed.
- Add the remaining cleansing substances to your daily regime (see the guidelines in this chapter).

### Personalized programme

- Continue with the personalized programme cleansing substances that you may have started last week.

- Add any other remaining cleansing substances that you are using.

*Refer back to Chapter Ten for how to take these supplements.*

## Energy exercises

- Practise the joint opening and grounding sequence for 20 minutes each day.
- Integrate belly breathing into your daily schedule.

## Lifestyle projects

- Continue skin brushing for 5 minutes every day.
- Follow skin brushing with the hot and cold shower routine.
- Take at least 15 minutes light exercise each day.
- Follow the guidelines on page 111 for creating a pollution-free home (optional).
- Treat yourself to a sauna or steam bath (optional).

## Other things in this chapter

- If needed, try the headache relief massage on page 112.

## Eating guidelines for Weeks Two and Three

During the second and third weeks of the programme you will be making your diet slightly more alkaline-forming, which means you need to reduce the amount of protein foods and grains you eat and increase your vegetables and fruits.

Menu plans for both the summer and winter months start on page 136 and you can follow these exactly or modify them according to your needs. They're completely vegetarian, but you can have a small amount of fish if you like.

If you choose to modify the menu plans, here are the guidelines you need to follow:

## Fruit

- Eat at least two pieces of fruit each day, more if possible.
- In the winter, don't keep fruits in the fridge, and lightly stew them before eating.
- Don't eat bananas at all.

## Vegetables

- Eat at least two large portions of vegetables each day, more if possible.
- Eat vegetables raw in the summer and add a handful of sprouting seeds to your salads.
- Cook vegetables during the winter (lightly stir-fried, steamed or baked).

## Grains

- Have a portion of brown rice at least every other day.
- Alternate this with a portion of other grains – millet is alkaline-forming and extremely beneficial.

## Pulses (legumes)

- You can have a small portion of chickpeas (including hummus) every day.
- You can also have a portion of other pulses (legumes) such as kidney beans or lentils every other day.

## Fish

- It's best if you can stick to a completely vegetarian diet during Weeks Two and Three, but everybody has different nutritional needs, so if you really find it hard to do without fish, you can have up to two portions a week during these two weeks. Salmon, herring, mackerel and halibut are the least acid-forming fish, so these are the best ones to have.

## Meat

- Avoid completely during Weeks Two and Three.

## Vegetarian protein

- Have a portion of live dairy-free yogurt every day.
- You can have tofu (bean curd) every other day.
- Don't eat any eggs at all.

## Nuts and seeds

- Eat a small handful of almonds and Brazil nuts every day, but don't eat any other nuts.
- Nibble a small handful of seeds (e.g. pumpkin, sunflower or sesame) every day.

## Fats

- As last week, you can use 1–2 tablespoons oil a day.

## The Detox Drink

To make the detox drink, freshly juice the following and drink immediately:

5 large carrots
2 celery stalks
1 small raw beetroot (beet)

These three vegetables are all highly alkalizing; they also support the whole elimination system. Carrots are high in the antioxidant beta-carotene and support the health of the digestive tract; beetroot (beet) is beneficial for the liver, gall bladder, lymph and kidneys, is high in powerful antioxidants called anthocyanidins (mentioned in Chapter Thirteen) and has traditionally been used as a blood-building food; celery is particularly beneficial for the kidneys and the lymph, it helps the body excrete excess fluid and it also provides a rich source of minerals needed by the body's buffering systems to remove acid from the tissues and blood.

## Adding the cleansing substances

### 1 The psyllium drink

Mix 1 tablespoon psyllium powder with a small amount of water, stir thoroughly and drink straightaway (otherwise it turns into a gel). Drink a medium-sized glass of water immediately afterwards. It's extremely important to have the second glass of water because the psyllium needs the extra fluid to make it swell properly as it passes through your digestive tract.

*(If you have chosen to take psyllium in capsule form, 4 capsules are about equivalent to 1 tablespoon powder. Take them with a large glass of water.)*

When to take the psyllium drink

- For the first three days of Week Two, have one psyllium drink a day.
- For the remainder of Week Two and the first four days of Week Three, have two psyllium drinks a day (one in the morning and one at night).
- For the final three days of the detox in Week Three, revert back to one psyllium drink a day.

You can take the psyllium drink at any time of day, but it must be taken on an empty stomach, so about half an hour before your main meals (lunch and dinner) is ideal. On the days when you are having two psyllium drinks, take one in the morning and one in the evening.

### 2 Milk thistle

Choose any good-quality milk thistle supplement containing 100–200mg of the herb and take one tablet with breakfast, along with your multivitamin.

### 3 MSM

You need to take 2 grams a day. If you have bought the powdered version, 2 grams is equivalent to ½ teaspoon. Mix it into a little water and take it at any time of day that suits you best.

## 4 Vitamin C

Take 1 gram (1000mg) vitamin C a day with food, at any meal.

## Personalized programme

Continue with the additional components for the stomach and intestines that you started last week. You also need to add any additional cleansing substances to your programme for this and the following week. The details of how to take these were given in Chapter Ten.

## Energy exercise – joint opening and grounding sequence

This exercise is based on *chi gung*, a very powerful system of working with energy that originated in China. The joint opening sequence helps to open up the channels that your body energy flows through, and it also helps the body to mobilize and remove waste materials that have accumulated in the joint areas. The grounding part of the exercise is excellent for building up your vitality and for balancing yourself whenever you feel stressed, scattered or hyper. Do the joint opening sequence first, then do the grounding exercise followed by the closing sequence.

The key to getting the most out of this is to focus your mental attention on the part of the body you are working on – really concentrate on the sensations you experience as you move a specific part of your body. If you can (and the weather is warm enough), practise this exercise barefoot on the grass, but doing it inside is okay as well. The instructions may appear quite long, but the exercise is actually quite straightforward, and the whole sequence should only take about 20 minutes.

### The basic body position

- Feet are hip-width apart and pointing straight ahead. Your weight should be equally distributed between both feet.
- Knees need to be slightly bent.
- Pelvis should be slightly tucked in.
- Spine is straight.

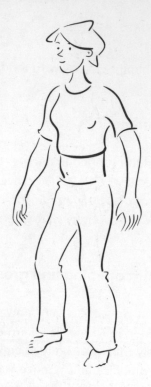

- Head is upright.
- Arms are relaxed and hanging loosely by the sides of the body.
- Keep your eyes open with a slight focus towards the ground.
- Keep your body relaxed throughout the sequence.

## The joint opening sequence

- Start from the basic body position above.
- Lift your left leg so your foot is about 5cm/2in off the floor.
- Rotate your left ankle clockwise 10 times, then rotate it anti-clockwise 10 times.
- Repeat with your right ankle.
- Grab both knees with your hands and rotate your knees 10 times in a clockwise circular movement (as if you are drawing an invisible horizontal circle with each knee), then rotate them 10 times in an anti-clockwise movement.

- Stand up straight again and lift your left leg off the ground by about 30cm/12in, bending your knee at a 90-degree angle. Rotate the leg clockwise 10 times (as if you are drawing a vertical circle in the air with your knee), then rotate it anti-clockwise a further 10 times. You should feel this movement primarily in the hip joint. Repeat with the right leg.

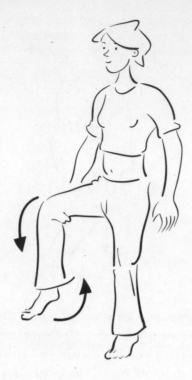

- Move your pelvis in a clockwise circular movement 10 times, then repeat in an anti-clockwise direction. Perform this movement very slowly (it's identical to the pelvic dance movement done in calypso, soca and salsa, except much slower).
- In one fluid continuous movement, twist the top half of your body to the left, then back to the middle and then to the right. Your head should follow the movement of your spine, so you will be looking to the left and right. Allow your arms to hang loose and follow the twisting movement so they swing with it and gently tap your middle back at the furthest point of the motion. Repeat 20 times. The movement originates from your waist so your hips and pelvis should remain stationary and the legs solid.
- Make a circular movement with your shoulders. Repeat 10 times in each direction.
- Move your head to the left, back to the middle, then to the right in a slow, continuous sequence while the rest of your body remains still and relaxed. Repeat 10 times.

## The grounding exercise

- Assume the basic body position, remembering to keep your knees slightly bent.
- Pay attention to your feet, feeling the connection between them and the ground, and take a few slow, deep belly breaths.
- Imagine your feet have roots like a tree and they're starting to descend deep into the earth. (If you are doing this exercise inside, just visualize your roots descending through the floors of the building and then going into the earth.)
- Feel any tension or scattered feelings roll down your body through your feet and imaginary roots into the earth.
- Remain in this position for a couple of minutes. Keep breathing slowly and deeply and try to remain connected to the sensations you're feeling in your body. Continue to feel yourself sinking and connecting deeper with the earth.
- When you have let go of emotional and physical tension and have fully connected to the earth, you should feel very calm and centred. In this state you are connecting to your own unique inner strength and capacity for joy. You are also connecting strongly to nature.
- As you are in the grounding position you may notice your legs starting to tremble slightly, or you may feel a tingling in them. You may also start to feel hot. All these sensations are good – they're indicating that energy is flowing through your body. You should now notice that you're feeling very invigorated and energized, but calm and relaxed at the same time.
- Don't worry if you don't get these sensations; they will probably come when you practise the exercise more often.


## Completing the exercise

- You are still in the basic body position.
- Inhale slowly, lifting both arms above your head in a semi-circle as you inhale.
- Exhale slowly, lowering your arms back to your sides at the same time.
- Repeat 3 times.

## Using the grounding sequence to re-balance yourself

Once you're familiar with the grounding part of this exercise it can be used throughout the day whenever you feel you need it, and the good thing is you don't have to be in a standing position to do it. If you're having a tough day at work, the following simple exercise will quickly break the build-up of a stress cycle, and it can be done in a couple of minutes while you're sitting at your desk.

- Take a couple of slow belly breaths and focus your attention inside your body.
- Using the power of your mind, feel yourself gradually and gently grounding down into the earth.
- Focus on your feet and feel yourself slowly and gently sinking back into your body and connecting to nature.
- Imagine that any stress you are feeling slides off your body, through your feet and into the ground.

## Integrating belly breathing into your daily schedule

Making belly breathing your normal style of breathing can bring a multitude of benefits, including greater energy levels and better resilience to stress. It also promotes digestive health because you're giving your digestive organs an 'internal massage' with each breath. Having become familiar with this form of breathing during the previous week, you can now take a few simple steps to integrate it more fully into your daily life – ideally you should belly breathe all of the time.

Try to get into the habit of breathing from the belly while you're doing your usual day-to-day activities; you don't have to do the counting or focus on the energy component. Here are some suggestions for good times to practise.

- When you're waiting to be served at the supermarket, bank or post office.
- Whenever you're stuck in traffic (it will keep your stress levels down).
- While you're watching TV.

- Doing household chores for which you need to stand still – like doing the dishes and ironing.
- Travelling to and from work.

Any time you feel yourself getting stressed or agitated, take a couple of minutes away from whatever you're doing and just belly breathe (and add the grounding sequence). This is an excellent way of short-circuiting a stress cycle.

## Hot and cold shower routine

This shower is a good way of stimulating all your elimination systems – it helps to move lymph fluid in particular – and it can also strengthen the immune system. It's best done in the summer, but if you feel like doing it in the winter, make sure your home is warm so you don't catch a chill. The very best time to do it is straight after skin brushing in the morning.

First run the shower at a reasonably warm, comfortable temperature. Don't run it too hot because there's no point in this – the benefit comes from the cold water.

- Once your body is accustomed to the warm temperature, turn it down to cold for about 20 seconds. The shock of the cold water cascading on to your body will probably make you want to scream or shout. Allowing yourself to make some noise is actually beneficial as it keeps your energy flowing.
- Now switch the temperature back to hot again for about a minute.
- Repeat this sequence three or four times.

## Exercise

To support your elimination system, continue taking at least 15 minutes exercise a day, or more if you feel like it. Swimming and walking are ideal, but avoid anything too strenuous in the gym.

## Creating a pollution-free home (optional)

We can't really control our exposure to pollutants when we are out and about, but we can at home. Here are a few ideas:

- Don't cook in aluminium pots and pans; use stainless steel.
- Don't use antiperspirants or deodorants that contain aluminium. Buy an aluminium-free one at the health food store.
- Reduce your exposure to plastics such as cling film (plastic wrap) and plastic food containers, and don't put hot food into plastic containers (plastics can interfere with hormone balance in both men and women).
- Don't use strong cleaning chemicals, especially aerosol sprays.
- Keep the windows open when you're cleaning.
- Sleep with the window slightly open so fresh air circulates continually.
- Have at least one houseplant in all the main areas of your home.
- Invest in an ioniser for your home (and your office). It helps suck pollutants out and pumps negative ions in, which will have a positive effect on your energy levels.

## Sauna or steam bath (optional)

A sauna or steam bath once or twice a week is an excellent addition to your detox programme because the heat helps the whole elimination system, particularly the lymph and skin. Saunas are also a great place to unwind and release stress that has accumulated during the day, and the warming effect is especially beneficial during the winter months. Here are a few tips:

- If you're not used to taking saunas, start gradually.
- Stay in for a maximum of five minutes, then have a cold shower and rest for a couple of minutes.
- Go back in for another five minutes.
- You will get the most benefit if you stay in for short periods and have frequent cold showers, but as you get used to it you can stay in for a little longer.
- Drink plenty of water afterwards, to replenish the fluid lost in sweat.

## Headache relief massage

Spending a couple of minutes doing this massage is often a highly effective way of relieving a headache and it's much better than adding strain to your liver by taking tablets. Breathe deeply and slowly through your mouth while you're doing all the massage points and, if you're in an appropriate place, it's also helpful to make sounds such as a slow, deep 'ahhhhh' as you exhale. Here goes ...

- Place each of your middle fingers just above your cheekbone exactly parallel to your eyes and about 2.5–5cm/1–2in away.
- Massage for 1 minute, using a reasonably firm circular motion.
- Move your thumbs along the underside of the bone that is just above the eye socket where your eyebrows are. Locate the ridge near to where the eye socket meets the top of your nose (your eyes should be closed). When you find a point that has a small indentation, you've found the right spot.
- With a *very* gentle pressure, press your thumbs into this point. Hold for 10 seconds, then release.
- Repeat three or four times.
- Now move your middle fingers to the back of your skull and find the point where the top of your spine/neck meets the bottom of your skull.
- Use a circular massage movement around this area for one minute.
- Place all your fingers on the top part of your skull and massage gently for another minute.

After finishing the massage, stand up and move your body around for about a minute. Use any movement you feel like, such as swinging your arms around, gyrating your shoulders or wiggling your hips. This helps your circulation, which can also alleviate the headache.

| DAILY DETOX ACTIVITIES | | | | | | | |
|---|---|---|---|---|---|---|---|
| **Week Two** | Day 1 | Day 2 | Day 3 | Day 4 | Day 5 | Day 6 | Day 7 |
| *Skin brushing* | | | | | | | |
| *Hot/cold shower* | | | | | | | |
| *Lemon juice* | | | | | | | |
| *Flaxseeds* | | | | | | | |
| *Multivitamin* | | | | | | | |
| *Vitamin C* | | | | | | | |
| *Milk thistle* | | | | | | | |
| *Psyllium* | | | | | | | |
| *2nd psyllium*\* | | | | • | • | • | • |
| *MSM* | | | | | | | |
| *Detox drink* | | | | | | | |
| *Water* | | | | | | | |
| *Multimineral* | | | | | | | |
| *Joint opening and grounding exercises* | | | | | | | |
| ***Personal:*** | | | | | | | |
| | | | | | | | |
| | | | | | | | |
| | | | | | | | |
| | | | | | | | |
| | | | | | | | |

\*Only have the second psyllium drink on days 4–7 of this week

## chapter 16

# Super Energy Detox Week Three

## Things to do this week

### Diet

- Continue with the freshly squeezed lemon juice and water when you get up.
- Continue adding 1 tablespoon ground flaxseeds to your breakfast cereal or juice.
- Continue with 1 glass of Detox Drink (page 101) every day.
- Continue with 1½ litres/1½ quarts water (filtered or mineral) every day.
- The eating plan for this week is the same as in Week Two.
- Continue with all the recommendations given in the previous chapter.

### Supplements

- Continue with the supplementation programme you were following in Week Two.
- Have only one psyllium drink a day during the last three days of this week.

### Personalized programme

- Continue as you were doing in Week Two.

## Energy exercises

- Continue with the joint opening and grounding sequence for 20 minutes each day.
- Have fun experimenting with the *Chi* ball exercise (below).
- Practise Breath of fire (page 116) for 1–2 minutes each day.
- Continue integrating belly breathing into your daily schedule so this breathing pattern becomes the norm.

## Lifestyle projects

- Continue skin brushing for 5 minutes every day.
- Continue with the hot and cold shower routine.
- Take at least 15 minutes exercise each day, more if you can.
- Do the energizers and depleters exercise (optional, but highly recommended).
- Treat yourself to a lymphatic drainage massage (optional).

## Other things in this chapter

- Ending the detox.

# Energy exercises

### 1 *Chi* ball

The best time to practise this is just after you've completed the joint opening and grounding sequence when your energy will be quite high and vibrant, but feel free to practise it whenever it suits you.

- Do this exercise either standing up (in the basic body position from the joint opening sequence) or sitting in a chair. If you're sitting, make sure your back is straight and your feet are placed firmly on the floor.
- Rub the palms of your hands together vigorously for about 30 seconds.
- Cup your hands very slightly and move them about 60cm/2 feet

apart with your palms facing each other. Bend your arms at a 90 degree angle so your hands are parallel with your diaphragm muscle.

- Very, very slowly start to bring your hands closer together (it can help to keep your eyes closed as you are doing this).
- Focus on the sensations you feel in the palms of each hand.
- As your hands move closer together – usually when they are about 10cm/4in apart – you should start to feel sensations of heat or tingling. You should also notice a spongy feeling between your hands, as if something solid is there.
- Try to get a clearer sensation of the solid substance by moving your hands around it as if you are playing with an invisible tennis ball. Play with it for as long as your attention can remain focused on it.
- If you lose the sensation, take a couple of deep belly breaths and start again. Rub your palms together, then move your hands further apart and bring them closer together again.
- You can make the energy of the ball stronger by focusing your attention on your breath – as you exhale imagine that energy is flowing through your arms, out of your hands and into the ball, which should now feel larger and more solid.
- When you are ready to end the exercise, place your palms over the lower part of your abdomen and take a couple of deep breaths. You may notice heat or a tingling sensation as the energy of the *chi* ball is absorbed into your body.
- To complete the exercise, shake your arms vigorously for a few seconds and rub the soles of your feet on the floor.

This exercise gives you a tangible experience of energy rather than keeping it merely as an abstract concept, because the solid, spongy substance that you felt between your hands is actually *your own energy*. Your first *chi* ball may be about the size of a tennis ball and feel quite fragile, but if you practise the exercise regularly you will be able to build larger and more solid energy balls.

## 2 Breath of fire

This is a highly invigorating breathing exercise that also helps the detox process. You can do it at any time of day, but it is *very important* to have an empty stomach, so before meals is ideal. It consists of panting breaths done in rapid succession – about one second for each combined inhale and exhale. As you exhale, your diaphragm muscle contracts inwards and this should happen automatically, but you can help the process by lightly squeezing the muscle. During the inhale you don't have to do anything, because the diaphragm relaxes automatically.

*Breathe only through your nose throughout the whole of this exercise.*

- Sit down in either a cross-legged position on the floor or, if you find this uncomfortable, on a chair. Make sure your back is straight and the clothing around your waist is loose.
- Exhale reasonably forcefully (but without straining), as if you are trying to blow out a candle – a sharp, powerful and quick exhalation.
- Relax. You don't need to actively inhale as it happens automatically (due to the fact you've created a vacuum in your lungs during the exhale).
- Repeat the exhale-inhale sequence 10 times in rapid succession (which should take about 10 seconds). Stop, then take 4 slow rhythmic belly breaths.
- Repeat the same sequence a further 10 times followed by 4 slow breaths.
- This is the maximum you should do the first time you practise this exercise.

Do this exercise each day for a maximum of 1 minute. It's a powerful exercise so you should practise it with caution – only do as much as you feel comfortable with and definitely avoid straining or forcing yourself. Stop if you feel dizzy. Build up to a maximum of 20 rapid breaths and 4 slow breaths per sequence, with a total of three sequences. Don't go beyond this level.

## Energizers and depleters (optional)

While diet and exercise are important for maintaining your energy levels, what is happening in your emotional life also has an equally strong influence. Recall the last time you fell in love: chances are that you were bubbling with energy and vitality even though you were having late nights and not getting sufficient sleep. Perhaps you can also recall a time when you were really excited about your job – you woke up in the morning keen and eager to seize the day and you could work long hours without feeling tired.

During these periods the strong, positive emotions you were experiencing were having a tangible physical effect on your energy levels. These type of feelings flood your body with endorphins, the 'happy-hormones' that eliminate stress, boost the immune system and promote high energy levels. Conversely, when we are having a difficult time with life, endorphin production is reduced and replaced by the energy-depleting stress hormones.

While major life issues such as relationship difficulties can obviously cause stress, minor day-to-day problems can also have a substantial depleting effect. These daily hassles – things like household chores, frequent problems with childcare, worries about an elderly relative and endless traffic jams – are often more debilitating than major life events because they occur on a regular basis and are on-going over a long period of time.

If you don't manage to balance the energy-depleters with a sufficient level of energy-boosting activities, life will lose its sparkle and your energy levels will not be all they could be. Following the healthiest diet and exercise regime won't provide you with that much benefit when you are bogged down with too many depleting activities, so when you are coming to the end of the detox it's useful to spend a little time evaluating your life in this fashion.

It's beyond the scope of this book to give you specific strategies for dealing with life's stresses, but what this particular exercise can do is provide you with a framework for getting your energizers and depleters into a healthy balance. It's useful to look at energizers in two ways: there are invigorating energizers that make you feel excited and alive and provide you with lots of fun, and there are calming energizers that make you feel happy, contented and relaxed. We all need plenty of both types if our lives are to be in a healthy balance.

To do this exercise, set aside at least an hour when you know you won't be disturbed. You will need a pad of paper and a pen.

## Your depleters

- Make a list of all of the activities currently in your life that make you feel grumpy, irritable or depressed, including activities that give you a sinking feeling by just thinking about them.
- Reflect upon your underlying reasons for choosing these activities. Many of our depleters consist of 'shoulds', such as 'I really *should* see this friend once a week because I've known her since we were little, but I do find her company very depressing'. In this example, you will be doing both yourself and the friend a favour by limiting contact, and by recognizing that you don't really have to do a particular depleting activity, you will give yourself permission to drop it from your life.
- Outline strategies for eliminating your depleters. Can you delegate tasks to someone else (who might actually enjoy them)? Can you restructure your working hours so you miss the rush hour or do the food shopping during off-peak times? There are always solutions to any situation, so allow yourself to be creative and 'step out of the box' to come up with novel answers.
- Change your outlook towards your depleters. This is especially important for activities you feel you have to do. What's important is the attitude we bring to an activity rather than the activity itself. Doing the housework can be an irritating, depleting chore or an enjoyable task depending on your attitude to it. Put on some funky music and dance while you're vacuuming, or make housework a game for the children by offering a treat for the one who tidies their room first.

## Your invigorating energizers

- Make a list of at least 10 activities (more if possible) that make you feel really alive, vibrant and energized when you do them – activities you look forward to and that fill you with enthusiasm when you think about doing them.
- What you find invigorating and energizing will be unique to your individual personality – it may be dancing, going out with friends, shopping, a sport such as swimming, water-skiing or horse riding,

going to a concert, being in a debating society or travelling abroad. Whatever it is, participating in your favourite activity (and thinking about doing it), makes you feel positive, happy and 'up'.

• How often do you do these favourite things? Think about ways in which you can do them more frequently – which of your invigorating energizers can you do on a daily basis or at least once a week?

## Your calming energizers

• These activities differ from the invigorating ones because they make you feel happy and positive at the same time as promoting a sense of calm and relaxation. Calming energizers are important, because they are a powerful way of recharging your energy levels.
• Make a list of at least 10 activities that can make you feel this way. Examples may be lying down and hugging your partner or child, watching your favourite movie, listening to classical music (or any relaxing music that you find inspiring), staying in bed all morning, soaking in a bubble bath, having a massage, reading a good book, walking in the country, meditating, practising breathing exercises and making love (love-making can be very invigorating but the after effect is usually calming and relaxing).
• How often do you give yourself permission to do these activities? Which can you easily find time to do more often? Which can you do on a daily basis?
• Commit to giving yourself time to have at least one calming energizer each day.

## Lymphatic drainage massage

If you fancy giving yourself a real pampering and energizing treat, try a lymphatic drainage massage – it's different from a standard body massage in that it involves specific massage strokes which shift and move your lymph fluid, and it's particularly useful if you suffer with cellulite and fluid retention. Lymphatic drainage massage is quite a specialized treatment and it may not be available everywhere, so if you can't find a local practitioner, enjoy a normal massage instead.

## Ending the detox

The way in which you end a detox is as important as the detox itself. All your hard work and effort can be ruined if you end up grabbing a takeaway burger and chips, and doing something like this could also make you feel quite unwell because your digestive system hasn't been used to this kind of food for the past few weeks. Your body is now also used to living without coffee, tea, alcohol, refined sugar and the like, and it will be highly sensitive to them. Before the detox you might have had four or five cups of coffee a day without noticing any effect, but after the detox one cup of coffee could leave you feeling very hyped-up.

Hopefully, by the end of the detox, you won't want to rush out for takeaways and guzzle endless cups of coffee: by the end of Week Three you should be feeling great and in tune with your body's rhythms and needs, and this will help you make healthy diet and lifestyle choices in the long term. To help you with this, I suggest you follow the dietary principles from Week One for a further week before re-introducing harder-to-digest things like fried foods, which should be kept to a minimum in the longer term.

You should now stop taking the nutritional supplements and cleansing substances, but you can continue with the multivitamin, multimineral and vitamin C supplements if you want to – they're a useful addition to a healthy diet. You can also finish off any remaining flaxseeds, as these will turn rancid if not used within a short period of time, but the psyllium husk, milk thistle and MSM can be stored until your next detox. If you're following the guidelines for the intestines and food intolerance programme, you will continue taking the intestinal supplements for a few more months (see the next chapter). The probiotic supplement needs to be used or it will lose its potency within a couple of months.

Many of the dietary strategies you've followed during the past three weeks can be incorporated into your usual daily routine. Regular vegetable juices provide numerous benefits to your health, so try not to let the dust settle on your juicer, and the new healthy and nutritious foods you've been introduced to (such as the gluten-free grains, quinoa and seeds) can continue to be part of your diet. In fact, the guiding principles of the detox (discussed in Chapter Eight) can give you a framework for a healthy diet in the long term – if you want to support your health, aim to eat lots of alkaline-forming foods as a way of life rather than just for the detox period.

The same thing applies to the energy exercises that you've experimented with during the past few weeks. Regularly practising the joint opening sequence can keep your energy levels high and reduce the risk of joint aches and pains or arthritis in later life. If you enjoyed these exercises, you may also want to explore such things as *chi gung* and yoga classes.

The end of the detox is also a good time to re-take the questionnaires and indicators given in Chapters Four and Nine, as these will let you make further evaluations of the changes that have occurred to your well-being. It's amazing how quickly we forget that we used to frequently suffer from a particular complaint, so re-taking the tests can act as a memory jogger.

If you feel like it, you can do another detox in a few months' time – a regular detox once or twice a year can definitely support your health and well-being. Provided your diet remains healthy (i.e. not too much sugar, alcohol, refined foods and stimulants), and any food intolerance problems are dealt with adequately, you can skip the 'lightening your load' week and go straight into the detox itself. You may also want to explore deeper detox strategies such as juice fasts and colon cleansing programmes (including colonic irrigation).

The detox programme should have given you some clear indications whether you are experiencing a food intolerance condition or not. If you are, it's likely that you experienced some improvements in your well-being (such as increased energy and less bloating) by the end of the first week, but three weeks is insufficient time to deal with a food intolerance problem adequately. If intolerance is present, you will benefit from following the maintenance programme outlined in the next chapter.

| DAILY DETOX ACTIVITIES | | | | | | | |
|---|---|---|---|---|---|---|---|
| **Week Three** | Day 1 | Day 2 | Day 3 | Day 4 | Day 5 | Day 6 | Day 7 |
| *Skin brushing* | | | | | | | |
| *Hot/cold shower* | | | | | | | |
| *Lemon juice* | | | | | | | |
| *Flaxseeds* | | | | | | | |
| *Multivitamin* | | | | | | | |
| *Vitamin C* | | | | | | | |
| *Milk thistle* | | | | | | | |
| *Psyllium* | | | | | | | |
| *2nd psyllium\** | • | • | • | • | | | |
| *MSM* | | | | | | | |
| *Detox drink* | | | | | | | |
| *Water* | | | | | | | |
| *Multimineral* | | | | | | | |
| *Exercise* | | | | | | | |
| *Joint opening and grounding exercises* | | | | | | | |
| *Breath of fire Chi ball* | | | | | | | |
| ***Personal:*** | | | | | | | |
| | | | | | | | |
| | | | | | | | |
| | | | | | | | |
| | | | | | | | |

*Only have the second psyllium drink on days 1–4 of this week

## chapter 17

# The Maintenance Programme

The detox programme is a great first step towards overcoming a food intolerance problem – it needn't be a lifelong sentence. It's possible, indeed relatively easy, to strengthen the underlying body systems involved in an intolerance condition in such a way that offending foods can eventually be reintroduced without health problems re-occurring. However, it generally takes longer than three weeks to deal with this condition adequately, so this chapter provides you with a structured programme to help deal with the condition in the longer term.

## Determining your needs

Having completed the detox, one of two conditions will apply to you.

First, you may have found out that you had an intolerance to a certain food as a result of doing the elimination trial before the detox or from seeking professional support. In this case you should have a clear knowledge and understanding of which foods are associated with your health problems.

Second, you may have decided to follow the detox programme before confirming whether or not you had an intolerance. As I mentioned in Chapter Four, using the detox as a way of determining whether intolerance is present is not ideal. Any health changes that you have experienced may be indicators of food intolerance, but you have made many other changes to your diet and lifestyle during the past three weeks and so it's difficult to ascertain whether any improvements to your health and well-being are the direct result of removing an intolerant food or the other changes.

If you didn't do the elimination trial or have your intolerance condition properly tested, I recommend you do a retest trial before embarking on the maintenance programme, because the programme necessitates avoiding any offending foods for a few months.

*There is absolutely no value in eliminating a specific food from your diet unless you have a genuine intolerance condition.*

This is an important point. There's a lot of hype surrounding food intolerance – it sometimes even appears to be a 'trendy' condition to suffer from. There has been no large-scale scientific study that has accurately identified the percentage of the population who suffer from intolerance (such a study would pose numerous methodological problems), but should there ever be one, I suspect that the actual incidence of genuine intolerance cases would be far less than expected.

This doesn't mean your symptoms are 'all in the mind', but it's a fact that sometimes we assume we have an intolerance to a specific food when in fact our symptoms may equally well relate to an overburdened elimination system.

As discussed in Chapter Two, modern diet and lifestyle put a great deal of strain on our elimination systems – a diet high in acid-forming foods, stimulants, alcohol and the like can provoke a whole range of symptoms such as lack of energy, frequent headaches, poor skin and digestive disturbance, and these symptoms are similar in nature to those involved in food intolerance. To make sure you do have an intolerance before you embark on the maintenance programme, it's well worth taking a few days to complete a retest trial.

## The retest trial

This should give you pretty clear evidence as to whether or not a particular food is associated with any of your health problems.

- Choose to retest during a period when you know you're not going to be too busy – a weekend is usually ideal. Sometimes reintroducing a suspect food can provoke a reaction, so it's important to be able to rest if you need to.

- Test only one food at a time. Choose a food that contains only the ingredient you are testing. For example, if you are testing wheat, a pure-wheat cereal (that is sugar free) or plain pasta is a good choice. Bread is not a good choice as it contains other ingredients such as yeast. For dairy, try a glass of milk or a small piece of cheese (Edam or Cheddar is a good choice; don't try a blue cheese).
- Have a small meal containing only the test food. For example, have a pure wheat cereal with rice milk if you know that rice milk doesn't cause you any problems.
- Complete the pulse test (see below) and monitor your health during the next two to three days.
- Look out for a drop in energy levels (either shortly after eating the suspect food or any time over the next two days), or any re-occurrence of health problems (changes to bowel function in particular).
- If you don't experience any changes to your well-being within three days of testing the food (and the pulse test result was negative), then you are probably not intolerant to this food. In this case, it should be okay for you to reintroduce the food back into your diet.
- Some symptoms, like spotty skin for example, can take longer to emerge, so if you do reintroduce a food back into your diet, pay attention to this and any other symptoms that may occur during the following two to three weeks.
- If you noticed a negative change to your health and well-being (and the pulse test result was positive), you are probably intolerant to this food. In this case, you need to avoid this particular food in the short term and follow the maintenance programme.
- Wait for at least three days before testing another food.

## The pulse test

- Sit down and make sure you are as relaxed as possible.
- Measure your pulse.
- Eat the test food.
- Remain sitting down and relaxed.
- After about 10 minutes, measure your pulse again.

- Measure your pulse again after another 20 minutes has elapsed.

A significant change in your pulse rate – in the region of 20 beats per minute – can suggest that you are intolerant to the test food, and it generally occurs within half an hour of eating. Often the pulse rate increases when an intolerant food is eaten, but it's also possible for it to decrease.

The pulse test doesn't always provide accurate results: it's possible for your pulse to change even though you are not intolerant to a food (a false positive result), and it's also possible for your pulse to remain unchanged even though you are intolerant to the food (a false negative result). Therefore it's important not to determine your needs purely on the results of the pulse test alone. Instead, combine this result with any changes in your well-being over the next couple of days. If you get a clear indication from a change in your symptoms (such as diarrhoea or migraine), then you are probably intolerant to this particular food even if your pulse rate didn't change.

## The maintenance programme

This involves avoiding all your culprit foods at the same time as taking steps to improve the health and functioning of your elimination system (in particular by working with the digestive tract). This, of course, is what you've been doing during the past three weeks. The maintenance programme is therefore a direct extension of the detox programme you have just completed. How long you need to spend on the maintenance programme depends on your specific needs. Sometimes the body can respond very quickly so you may only need to avoid the culprit foods for about two months, but in general it may take closer to four months for reactions to certain foods to subside. These are the strategies you need to follow on the maintenance programme.

## Avoid culprit foods and eat healthy alternatives

While you're cutting out culprit foods, it's important to eat a healthy and balanced diet so you don't run the risk of developing nutritional deficiencies. Antoinette has provided you with plenty of recipes that don't contain the major culprit foods, so you shouldn't be short of ideas, and there are plenty of substitutes available at health food stores and supermarkets. These include wheat-free and gluten-free bread and pasta, plus many dairy alternatives such as goat's milk (and yogurt and cheese), soya milk and rice milk.

## Avoid anti-nutrients

As part of the strategy for supporting your digestive tract and liver, it's important to avoid anti-nutrients as much as possible. The major items to steer clear of are coffee, alcohol, chemical additives in food and pharmaceutical drugs, because these will put a strain on your liver and promote a leaky gut, undoing all the good work you are doing elsewhere. Your taste for these things has probably declined as a result of the detox anyway, but if you must have coffee or alcohol then try to keep to as little as possible. Other things to avoid include highly processed foods and any food that contains refined sugar.

## Balance your blood sugar

Many people who have a food intolerance condition also have unstable blood sugar, which can manifest itself as fluctuating energy levels throughout the day, or irritability and dizziness if food is not eaten frequently. These symptoms are often greatly alleviated once the culprit food is removed, but it's also important to take steps to strengthen your blood sugar mechanisms while following the maintenance programme.

The strategy for strengthening your blood sugar balance is quite simple: it involves eating foods containing lots of complex carbohydrates such as brown rice, the gluten-free grains (e.g. buckwheat and millet) and dried pulses (legumes) such as chickpeas and kidney beans. These foods release their energy quotient at a slow rate and therefore support a stable blood sugar. It's also important to eat regular meals, especially breakfast, and healthy snacks (such as fruits, nuts, seeds, and raw vegetables with hummus) between meals. Refined foods, which tend to dump glucose into the bloodstream very quickly, should be avoided.

## Variety in your diet

A balanced diet containing a healthy mix of complex carbohydrates, protein and fat should be followed while you're on the maintenance programme (and in the longer term too). Despite its bad name, dietary fat is important for liver health and numerous other important bodily functions, so eat oily fish (such as salmon and mackerel), nuts, seeds and small amounts of cold pressed vegetable oils as these are the best sources of healthy fats.

Aim to get as much variety into your diet as possible, because this will increase your chances of getting the complete spectrum of vitamins and minerals necessary to keep you in good health. Use this period as an opportunity to experiment with foods that you previously may not have eaten, and try out cuisines from different countries and cultures that you haven't tried before.

Everybody has unique dietary needs: there is no ideal diet that works for everyone. For example, some people feel very healthy on a vegan or vegetarian diet, while others feel unwell when they follow such a regime. All food has its place, provided it's fresh, unprocessed and not packed with chemicals. The key is to find the diet that suits your body, and the way to do this is to listen to the messages your body is giving you.

Having just completed the detox you should be much more aware of these messages. Before you prepare a meal, pause for a few seconds and connect with your body and emotions; make sure you are in a calm and centred emotional state and then ask yourself, 'If my body could talk what would it tell me to eat right now?' Listen to the answer – the image of a particular food may pop into your mind.

Then, after you've eaten, be aware of how you feel. Do you feel lethargic and heavy, or energized and clear-headed? These messages will give you very clear signals about the diet that is best for you, so trust your body and your instincts to make the right choice.

## Support the digestive system

The dietary principles just described will definitely help support the healing of your digestive system, but it's also beneficial to continue with the supplements you've been taking for the intestines during the detox.

The following supplements should be taken for 2–4 months.

- **Glutamine** to help heal a leaky gut.
  *Take 2 grams a day.*

- **FOS** to help promote the population of friendly bacteria that live in the gut.
  *Take 1–2 teaspoons a day.*

- **Probiotic supplement** as a source of friendly bacteria for the gut. Remember to keep this supplement in the fridge.
  *Take 1 tablet a day on an empty stomach.*

- **Anthocyanidins** are the powerful antioxidants found in berries, black grapes, black cherries and beetroots (beets) that support your immune system and help heal the gut wall. You can continue to get them directly from food and juices, as you were doing on the detox programme, or you can buy them in supplement form.
  *Take 1 tablet a day with food.*

- **Carrot juice** also promotes healing of the gut wall.
  *Drink a glass at least every other day as a useful addition to this programme.*

- **Flaxseeds** are a most valuable support for the digestive tract and they're also a good source of omega-3 fatty acids, which are often deficient in the diet (especially if fish is eaten infrequently).
  *Continue taking 1 tablespoon a day.*

- **Good multivitamin and multimineral supplements** ensure you're getting the full complement of nutrients.

## The longer term

After following this programme for a period of at least two months you may wish to retest a culprit food again. If you still react to it, continue on the programme for another month or two. After this length of time the great majority of intolerance sufferers find they're able to reintroduce the culprit food(s) back into the diet without getting negative reactions. If this isn't the case for you, you may need to avoid this particular food in the longer term. When you do reintroduce a previously intolerant food back into your diet, it's advisable not to eat more than moderate amounts.

Again, the key is to listen to the messages your body is giving you – once you've made a good connection with your body's communication system and followed its guidance you won't go far wrong.

I hope this detox programme has helped you reconnect to your body's wisdom and moved you further along the health spectrum.

A healthy and vibrant body is your birthright, so don't settle for anything less. Wishing you good health.

**Dawn Hamilton**

## chapter 18

# The Recipes

### Wheat allergies

The recipes in this book aim to use wheat-free ingredients but, as they are tailored primarily to readers who may not have a wheat allergy, they do include some ingredients, such as Worcestershire, Tabasco and soy sauce, baking powder and mixed spice (pie spice) or mustard, that contain tiny amounts of starch. For most people, these ingredients are fine in such small amounts, but must not be used by anyone with an allergy or severe intolerance to wheat. Items that may contain gluten are marked with an asterisk (*) in the ingredients column. Alternatives are easily purchased in good health food shops.

### Coeliacs

If you are a coeliac, you can use all the recipes in the book knowing that our nutritionist has checked every recipe. We have indicated any ingredient that does, or may, contain gluten with an asterisk (*) symbol, so that a gluten-free substitute can be purchased and used in the recipe.

### Yeast sensitivity

If you are sensitive to yeast, you can use all the recipes that are marked yeast-free knowing that our nutritionist has checked every recipe for you. Where possible, a suitable option has been indicated so that you can avoid ingredients that may contain yeast. Recipes containing sugar, honey or maple syrup, which can affect yeast sensitivity, have been indicated as not yeast-free.

## Measurements and other information

Throughout this book, all solid and liquid ingredients are given in metric and US measurements. Please use either one set or the other because the measures do not mix well. All recipes have been tested twice, using both measures. Eggs are medium unless specified as large.

All the recipes can be made with equipment found in most kitchens, but to ensure you do have everything required, any specific equipment, baking paper or other necessary items are listed in each recipe.

## Introduction

All the recipes in this part of the book will make starting and carrying through your new healthy eating plan easier. The recipes for the summer and winter detox programmes are featured within these pages, along with lots of irresistible seasonal dishes and ideas.

After completing the summer detox programme you can use the menu ideas devised for the summer season, knowing that you are eating the best of our seasonal produce created into mouthwatering recipes to suit all sorts of entertaining and family needs throughout the season.

In the same way, after completing the winter detox programme you can use the menu ideas devised for the winter season, knowing that keeping healthy will not mean that you are compromising on your lifestyle but instead benefiting from seasonal foods which comfort and warm the body and soul.

Most of the recipe introductions suggest alternative main ingredients, so the same dish can be made many times without anyone getting bored, least of all the cook!

For example, the halibut recipe on page 210 can be made with any white fish or oily fish such as salmon or tuna, depending on your budget or preference.

All the recipes are wheat-free; so if you do run out of wheat-free flour, do not be tempted to substitute with wheat flour. Make sure that you have plenty in the store cupboard.

Regular shopping at health food stores or supermarkets with a specialist health section is much better than the occasional panic-buying session; it's less hard work, the food is fresher, better for you and you can budget more easily.

Alternatively, you can order all the specialist items you need from the various mail-order companies listed at the back of the book. It is important to plan ahead at the best of times, but particularly when there are special occasions to cater for.

The white bread, white bread rolls and pizza base that are used in these recipes are part of the Antoinette Savill Signature Series of freshly baked foods, which are on sale in Waitrose and other supermarkets and health food stores in the UK. If you have access to the Internet you can also order them from the Waitrose website (www.waitrose.com), or by mail order from Wellfoods Ltd.

Any recipes that are not already dairy-free can be made so by substituting organic soya products in place of the dairy ingredients.

The menu suggestions, and the recipes themselves, are a good balance between vegetarian dishes and those with seafood, fish, poultry and meat. This not only achieves the best dietary and health results on the plan but also helps to keep the budgeting cost down. In fact, I think you will find that you recoup any additional expense of buying more fresh fruit, vegetables, nuts and seeds by eliminating the purchase of sweets (candies), chocolates, cookies, cakes and pastries.

If possible, do try to buy organic produce because I think it does have so much more flavour, and it is not packed full of pesticides and other chemicals. Also, free-range (farm fresh) eggs, poultry, game and meats are infinitely preferable as they not only have that old-fashioned homely taste of pre-mass production and freezing, but also do not contain additives and residues of chemicals.

Most of the recipes can easily be adapted for smaller or greater numbers. You can halve or double them (but do remember to change *all* the quantities!), so that your favourite dishes can be served to suit different occasions. The only exceptions are the roulades, cakes and puddings, but as they are only for entertaining and not part of the daily routine, this should suit your new lifestyle.

## Information

Here is some practical information to help you start and maintain your new eating plan. There is also a summer detox plan and a helpful list of menu suggestions to help guide you through Easter, picnics, barbecues and al fresco dining for the summer months. Also included are recipes for the lunch box and healthy snacks throughout the year. There is a winter detox plan and a helpful list of menu suggestions for lunches and dinners to get you through the rest of the year and be able to cope with Halloween, the Christmas and New Year festivities and even a romantic dinner for St Valentine's Day.

Before embarking on this new way of eating, it may help to make a list of things to do and to buy. As most people have to work during the week, the menu plans begin on Sunday, so that even the busiest person will be able to plan the week ahead and shop on Saturday.

You will find that the recipes can be easily adapted to use less expensive ingredients if necessary, and to your own personal likes and dislikes. These menus are only a helpful guide; so do swap things around to accommodate your schedule and lifestyle.

It is a good idea to have the recipes in front of you when you are making your shopping list, so that nothing is forgotten. Check the menu charts and see if you would like to change the recipes to suit your needs. You can make a given quantity and if it is too much, you can have it for lunch the next day.

## THE SUMMER DETOX PLAN

(For quick reference, photo-copy this list and fix to the refrigerator, desk or diary)
Recipes in this book are indicated by the following symbol: ★ consult the index to find them

## Week 1

| | Sunday | Monday | Tuesday | Wednesday | Thursday | Friday | Saturday |
|---|---|---|---|---|---|---|---|
| **BREAKFAST** *(Lemon, water and a little honey every day before breakfast)* | | | | | | | |
| | Millet flakes with dairy-free live yogurt & strawberries | Mixed berries (blueberries, cherries & strawberries) with dairy-free live yogurt | Blender fruit smoothie* | Mixed flakes with dairy-free milk & fresh fruit | Blender fruit smoothie* | Mixed berries (blueberries, cherries & strawberries) with dairy-free live yogurt | Mixed flakes with dairy-free milk & fresh fruit |
| **LUNCH** | | | | | | | |
| | Asparagus salad with coriander & ginger dressing* & a handful of sprouts | leftover Asparagus salad* & leftover Summer cooler soup* | Reduced fat hummus with raw vegetables of your choice & a handful of sprouts | Chilled avocado soup* cold brown rice & salad | Brown rice salad with grated raw vegetables, lemon juice & olive oil | Guacamole* (See recipe page 216) with raw vegetables of your choice & a handful of sprouts | Super summer mixed salad* |
| | Fresh fruit | Fresh fruit | Fresh fruit | Fresh fruit | Fresh fruit | Fresh fruit | Fresh fruit |
| **DINNER** | | | | | | | |
| | Summer cooler soup* Super summer mixed salad* & brown rice | Fusilli with roasted vegetables & olives* | Stir-fry vegetables of your choice with steamed brown rice | Brown rice with grated raw vegetables, lemon juice & olive oil | Large mixed salad with sprouts & a baked potato | Stir-fry vegetables of your choice with steamed brown rice | Vegetable kebabs with walnut & rice salad* fresh vegetables |
| | Fruit or fresh fruit salad | Fruit or fresh fruit salad | Fruit or fresh fruit salad | Fruit or fresh fruit salad | Fruit or fresh fruit salad | Fruit or fresh fruit salad | Fruit or fresh fruit salad |

## Weeks 2 and 3

| Sunday | Monday | Tuesday | Wednesday | Thursday | Friday | Saturday |
|---|---|---|---|---|---|---|
| **BREAKFAST** *(Lemon, water and a little honey every day before breakfast)* | | | | | | |
| Fresh papaya & pineapple with dairy-free live yogurt | Blender fruit smoothie* | Mixed flakes with dairy-free milk & fresh fruit | Mixed berries (blueberries, cherries & strawberries) with dairy-free live yogurt | Blender fruit smoothie* | Millet flakes with dairy-free live yogurt & strawberries | Mixed flakes with dairy-free milk & fresh fruit |
| **LUNCH** | | | | | | |
| Vegetable spring rolls* with your choice of stir-fry vegetables | Guacamole* (see recipe page 216) with raw vegetables of your choice | Summer cooler soup* & raw vegetable salad & a handful of sprouts | Reduced fat hummus with raw vegetables of your choice | Brown rice salad with grated raw vegetables, lemon juice & olive oil | Chilled avocado soup* & a mixed salad & a handful of sprouts | Super summer mixed salad* & brown rice |
| Water melon & lychee fruit salad | Fresh fruit | Fresh fruit | Fresh fruit | Fresh fruit | Fresh fruit | Fresh fruit |
| **DINNER** | | | | | | |
| Chilled avocado soup* & a mixed salad | Stir-fried tofu with large raw salad & some brown rice | Artichoke, butter bean & fennel salad* | Super summer salad* | Guacamole* large mixed salad, sprouts & brown rice | Vegetable kebabs with rice salad* | Fusilli with roasted vegetables & olives* |
| Fresh fruit or fresh fruit salad | Fresh fruit or fresh fruit salad | Fresh fruit or fresh fruit salad | Fresh fruit or fresh fruit salad | Fresh fruit or fresh fruit salad | Fresh fruit or fresh fruit salad | Fresh fruit or fresh fruit salad |

## Lunch and dinner ideas

Here are some menu suggestions using the recipes that will be at their best throughout the spring and summer

Prawn, Mango and Cucumber Salad*

Sesame Salmon Fingers with Sugar Snap Salad*

Fresh Pea Quiche* with vegetables or salad

Smoked Trout and Guacamole Rolls*

Chargrilled Squid with Herb Dressing* and salad

Penne with Trout, Fresh Peas and Lemon* with salad

Tomato and Pesto Tarts* with salad

Chilled Avocado Soup*
Roast Cod with Pineapple Salsa* and steamed green vegetables

Summer Cooler Soup*
Chicken Kiev in Parma Ham*
or Broad Bean and Spinach Frittata* with vegetables

Crispy Scallops with Pak Choi*
Chilled Halibut with Two Salsas*
Peach Angel Ring with Strawberry Coulis*

# Spring/summer special occasion menus

### Easter entertaining
*Menu for 6*
Coconut and Tomato Soup*
Rack of Lamb with Courgettes, Broad Beans and Mint*
(Vegetarian option: Cheese Roulade with Walnuts* and leeks)
Choice of fresh vegetables
Dark Chocolate Tart*

### Thai dinner
*Menu for 4*
Vegetable Spring Rolls*
Chicken and Basil Curry* with steamed fragrant Thai rice
*or*
Thai Fish Cakes with Lime Dipping Sauce*
Stir-fry vegetables of your choice
Mango sorbet (available at good supermarkets and stores)

### Summer party picnic
*Menu for 8*
Asparagus and Spinach Picnic Tart*
Chicken Liver and Cranberry Terrine with Broccoli and Almond Salad*
Tomato and basil salad
A mixed green leaf salad
Fusilli with Roasted Vegetables and Olives*
Lemon Muffins* with fresh strawberries and reduced-fat crème fraîche

### Summer barbecue
*Menu for 8*
Three Star Tostaditas*
Barbecued Vegetables with Dipping Sauce*
A Selection of salads
Raspberry and Pecan Roulade*

## THE WINTER DETOX PLAN

(For quick reference, photo-copy this list and fix to the refrigerator, desk or diary)
Recipes in this book are indicated by the following symbol: ★ consult the index to find them

## Week 1

| Sunday | Monday | Tuesday | Wednesday | Thursday | Friday | Saturday |
|---|---|---|---|---|---|---|
| BREAKFAST *(Lemon, water, ginger and a little honey every day before breakfast)* | | | | | | |
| Mixed grains with hot dairy-free milk | Stewed fruit (apples, pears or other fruit) & ginger & dairy-free yogurt | Cooked quinoa grains with cinnamon & ginger | Millet flakes & hot dairy-free milk & stewed fruit | Stewed fruit (apples, pears or other fruit) & ginger & dairy-free yogurt | Cooked quinoa grains with cinnamon & ginger | Mixed grains with hot dairy-free milk |
| LUNCH | | | | | | |
| Griddled sweet potatoes with three bean salad* | leftover Pasta & bean soup* | Brown rice, (hot), chopped cooked vegetables, olive oil & herbs | leftover Beetroot & cranberry soup* | Baked potato with hummus & salad | leftover Artichoke chowder* | Leeks napolitano* with winter vegetables |
| Fresh fruit | Fresh fruit | Fresh fruit | Fresh fruit | Fresh fruit | Fresh fruit | Fresh fruit |
| DINNER | | | | | | |
| Pasta & bean soup* (omit pancetta or bacon) | Winter Thai stir-fry* & steamed brown rice | Beetroot & cranberry soup* | Roast vegetables of your choice with brown rice | Artichoke chowder* | Stir-fry vegetables & tofu with brown rice | Large plate of steamed vegetables & brown rice Baked apples with spiced cranberry stuffing* |
| A winter fresh fruit salad or fruit | A winter fresh fruit salad or fruit | A winter fresh fruit salad or fruit | A winter fresh fruit salad or fruit | A winter fresh fruit salad or fruit | A winter fresh fruit salad or fruit | A winter fresh fruit salad or fruit |

## Weeks 2 and 3

| Sunday | Monday | Tuesday | Wednesday | Thursday | Friday | Saturday |
|---|---|---|---|---|---|---|
| BREAKFAST *(Lemon, water, ginger and a little honey every day before breakfast)* | | | | | | |
| Mixed grains with hot dairy-free milk | Stewed fruit (apples, pears or other fruit) & ginger & dairy-free yogurt | Cooked quinoa grains with cinnamon & ginger | Millet flakes & hot dairy-free milk & stewed fruit | Stewed fruit (apples, pears or other fruit) & ginger & dairy-free yogurt | Cooked quinoa grains with cinnamon & ginger | Mixed grains with hot dairy-free milk |
| LUNCH | | | | | | |
| Griddled sweet potatoes with three bean salad* | leftover Pumpkin soup* baked potato with hummus | Brown rice, (hot), chopped cooked vegetables, olive oil & herbs | leftover Fusilli with roasted vegetables & olives* | leftover Beetroot & cranberry soup* baked potato with hummus | Pasta & bean soup* (omit pancetta or bacon) | Griddled sweet potatoes with three bean salad* |
| Fresh fruit | Fresh fruit | Fresh fruit | Fresh fruit | Fresh fruit | Fresh fruit | Fresh fruit |
| DINNER | | | | | | |
| Pumpkin soup* brown rice, (hot) chopped cooked vegetables, olive oil & herbs | Winter Thai stir-fry* with steamed brown rice | Fusilli with roasted vegetables & olives* | Cranberry & beetroot soup* brown rice, (hot), chopped cooked vegetables, olive oil & herbs | Pasta & bean soup* | Winter Thai stir-fry* with steamed brown rice | Leeks napolitano* & brown rice with vegetables baked apples with spiced cranberry stuffing* |
| Winter fresh fruit salad or fresh fruit | Winter fresh fruit salad or fresh fruit | Winter fresh fruit salad or fresh fruit | Winter fresh fruit salad or fresh fruit | Winter fresh fruit salad or fresh fruit | Winter fresh fruit salad or fresh fruit | Winter fresh fruit salad or fresh fruit |

## Lunch and dinner ideas

Here are some menu ideas using the recipes that will be at their best throughout the autumn and winter.

Feta, Courgette and Tomato Pizza* with salad

Gingered Chicken Soup*

Winter Thai Stir-Fry* with steamed brown rice

Artichoke Chowder*
Swordfish Palermo* with vegetables

Pumpkin Soup with Creole Seeds*
Spiced Tuna on Noodles* with steamed vegetables

Oriental Smoked Salmon*
Chicken and Basil Curry* with stir-fried or steamed vegetables

Mushroom and Mozzarella Lasagne* with a mixed green salad
Blackberry and Apple Tartlets*

## Autumn (fall)/winter special occasion menus

### Christmas Day
*Menu for 8*
Pumpkin Soup with Creole Seeds*
Stuffed roast turkey with all the trimmings (substitute your traditional
    recipes with wheat/gluten-free breadcrumbs)
Vegetarian: Cheese Roulade with Walnuts* (decorate with holly)
Rosewater and Cinnamon Mince Pies*
Christmas pudding and brandy butter (see note below)
Fresh fruit and nuts

Note: There are recipes for gluten- and wheat-free stuffed roast turkey,
seasonal vegetables, Christmas pudding, cake, sauces and brandy butter
in the cookbook *The Gluten, Wheat and Dairy Free Cookbook* also
published by Thorsons.

### New Year's Eve
*Menu for 6*
Beetroot and Cranberry Soup*
Beef with Celeriac Mash, Tomato and Olive Compote*
with a selection of winter vegetables
Vegetarian: Mushroom and Mozzarella Lasagne*
A mixed continental salad
Prune, Almond and Cognac Tart*

### St Valentine's Day
*Menu for 2–4*
Sweet Red Pepper Dip*
Duck Breasts with Marmalade and Mango*
Roast winter vegetables
Passion Cakes with Passion Fruit Sauce*

## Ingredients

I have tried to make sure that the ingredients in this book are all available from the big supermarkets, but if you are not blessed with one close by, then a good health-food store should have all you need.

There is a list at the back of the book of companies who can provide mail order and delivery services.

The flour that is always used in all the recipes is wheat-free and gluten-free. It is available in the UK from Wellfoods Ltd (see addresses at the back) but is not available in America. Any other wheat-free and gluten-free flour will be suitable but, as the make-up of flour varies, you must allow for small adjustments to the liquid measurements if, when you make the recipe, it seems too dry or wet.

## Symbols used throughout this recipe section

**The following symbols are very important.** They are your guides to what is in each recipe. You can therefore use each recipe with complete confidence knowing that Dawn Hamilton has checked each recipe for you.

**GF**  suitable for coeliacs, gluten-free and wheat-free diets
**WF**  suitable for wheat-free diets but not gluten-free diets
**DF**  suitable for dairy-free and lactose-free diets
**V**  suitable for vegetarians
**YF**  suitable for yeast-sensitive people

Any one, or all of these symbols are printed at the top of each recipe. Please be sure that you are not intolerant or allergic to any other substance in the ingredients.

# Table of Contents

## Soups
Chilled avocado soup
Pumpkin soup with Creole seeds
Summer cooler soup
Coconut and tomato soup
Pasta and bean soup
Beetroot and cranberry soup
Gingered chicken soup

## Salads
Artichoke, butter bean and fennel salad
Asparagus salad with coriander and ginger dressing
Super summer mixed salad
Vegetable kebabs with walnut and rice salad
Prawn, mango and cucumber salad
Chicken liver and cranberry terrine with broccoli and almond salad
Sesame salmon fingers with sugar snap salad

## Vegetable and Vegetarian Dishes
Winter Thai stir-fry
Broad beans on lemon crostini
Tomato and pesto tarts
Vegetable spring rolls
Leeks Napolitano
Griddled sweet potatoes with three bean salad
Feta, courgette and tomato pizza
Lemon and spinach risotto
Fusilli with roasted vegetables and olives
Sweet red pepper dip
Cheese roulade with walnuts
Asparagus and spinach picnic tart
Coleslaw
Mushroom and mozzarella lasagne
Barbecued vegetables with dipping sauce
Broad bean and spinach frittata
Fresh pea quiche

## Fish and Seafood

Penne with trout, fresh peas and lemon
Smoked trout and guacamole rolls
Thai fish cakes with lime dipping sauce
Artichoke chowder
Swordfish Palermo
Crispy scallops with pak choi
Spiced tuna on noodles
Chargrilled squid with herb dressing
Chilled halibut with two salsas
Roast cod with pineapple salsa
Oriental smoked salmon
Three star tostaditas

## Meat and Poultry

Chicken Kiev in Parma ham
Rack of lamb with courgettes, broad beans and mint
Duck breasts with marmalade and mango
Beef with celeriac mash, tomato and olive compote
Chicken and basil curry
Chicken with rosemary and verjuice

## Desserts and Cakes

Dark chocolate tart
Baked apples with spiced cranberry stuffing
Rosewater and cinnamon mince pies
Lemon muffins
Passion cakes with passion fruit sauce
Prune, almond and cognac tart
Pumpkin pie
Raspberry and pecan roulade
Peach angel ring with strawberry coulis
Blackberry and apple tartlets
Blender fruit smoothie

**chapter 19**

# Soups

### Chilled Avocado Soup

This soup really does need to be chilled, and served within 2 hours, so that the amazing colour remains bright. It's lucky that it is so quick and easy to prepare!

*Serves 2 as a main course, or 3 as an appetizer*                    **GF WF DF V YF**

**Stock**

425ml (1¾ cups) vegetable stock or boiling water flavoured with 2 teaspoons of
   gluten-free vegetable bouillon powder* (yeast- and dairy-free are available)

**Salsa**

¼ small red onion, finely chopped

¼ red pepper and ¼ yellow pepper (bell pepper), seeded and finely chopped

2 heaped tablespoons coarsely chopped coriander (cilantro) leaves

7.5cm (3in) cucumber, peeled and finely chopped

1 tablespoon cold pressed extra virgin olive oil

2 teaspoons lemon juice

* Vegetable bouillon powder is gluten-free but if you decide to use other brands,
   do check for gluten.

**Soup**

2 large ripe avocados, halved, stoned (pitted) and all the flesh scraped out

2 tablespoons lemon juice

Chilli sauce*, paste* or minced in oil

Salt and freshly ground black pepper (don't use salt on detox)

First, make the vegetable stock and allow it to become cold.

- Make the salsa: mix the ingredients in the given order in a small bowl and toss until evenly coated. Cover and chill until ready to serve the soup.
- Now make the soup: put the avocado flesh into a blender, pour in the cold stock and blend until smooth. Pour the soup into a bowl; adjust the seasoning with the lemon juice, chilli, salt and pepper. Cover and chill. I usually shove it in the deepfreeze for 30 minutes.
- Divide the soup between the soup dishes and decorate with plenty of salsa. Serve immediately.

# Pumpkin Soup with Creole Seeds

I spent six months in the Hamptons, Long Island some years ago, and one of my favourite scenes was the pumpkin field in full bloom. I had never cooked a pumpkin before and was amazed at the variety of colours and sizes. Since then, every autumn (fall), I have enjoyed making this soup and a pumpkin pie for Halloween, just as I did years ago.

*Serves 6*                                                   **GF WF DF V YF**

1 large onion, finely chopped
2 tablespoons cold pressed extra virgin olive oil
2 garlic cloves, crushed
1 teaspoon cumin seeds
1 heaped teaspoon fresh thyme leaves
2 bay leaves
Sprinkling of freshly grated nutmeg
1 teaspoon ground allspice
Minced chilli in oil according to taste
1.5kg (3lb 5oz) pumpkin with top and bottom sliced off, quartered, peeled, seeds
   removed, and the flesh coarsely chopped
1.5 litres (6 cups) vegetable stock or 2 teaspoons of gluten-free vegetable bouillon
   powder dissolved in boiling water (yeast- and dairy-free are available)
Salt and freshly ground black pepper (don't use salt on detox)

### Creole seeds
1 teaspoon paprika
½ teaspoon ground cumin
½ teaspoon mixed spice* (pie spice)
60g (⅓ cup) pumpkin seeds
175g (1 cup) canned or frozen, unsweetened, sweetcorn kernels, drained or
   defrosted

Gently cook the onions in 1 tablespoon of oil in a large pan over a low heat until soft, but do not let them brown. Add the garlic, cumin seeds, thyme, bay leaves, nutmeg, allspice and chilli and stir together for 1 minute. Stir in the pumpkin, cover with the vegetable stock, and bring to the boil over a medium heat.

• Simmer the soup for about 40 minutes, or until the pumpkin is soft.

- Prepare the Creole seeds. Mix the paprika, ground cumin, mixed spice (pie spice) and the remaining oil together in a little bowl and toss the seeds in the mixture. Fry them in a non-stick pan with the sweetcorn for about 3–4 minutes or until dark brown at the edges.
- Leave the soup to cool and then purée in a blender until smooth. Transfer the soup back to the pan, reheat and season to taste with pepper. Stir in the hot Creole seeds and sweetcorn and serve immediately.

## Summer Cooler Soup

This soup is a triumph for those of us who prefer no-cooking recipes for summer dinner parties. When you are feeding fewer people, keep the soup chilled, then fill a thermos with some of the leftovers and take it to lunch with you over the next day or two.

*Serves 8*                                                    **GF WF DF V YF**

1 head crisp celery, carefully trimmed of leaves, root, blemishes and all tough fibres then coarsely chopped
1 litre (4 cups) organic, pure tomato juice
1 large firm cucumber, peeled and coarsely chopped
700ml (2¾ cups) organic, fresh or bottled carrot juice
1 small bunch spring onions (scallions) very finely chopped
1 large garlic clove, crushed
Chilli sauce* or minced chilli in vegetable oil
Juice of 1 lemon (or according to taste)
Salt and freshly ground black pepper (don't use salt on detox)
15g (½oz) fresh parsley, finely chopped

Purée the prepared celery with the tomato juice in a blender, at the highest speed, until smooth. Pour it into a big serving bowl. Purée the cucumber with the carrot juice until smooth and add to the tomato and celery juice mixture in the bowl.

- Sprinkle the soup with the spring onions (scallions), garlic, chilli and lemon juice and then stir and season to taste with salt and pepper.
- Cover and chill until needed. Serve the soup chilled in soup bowls and sprinkle with the parsley.

## Coconut and Tomato Soup

I made this by sheer accident one evening when I was rooting around the store cupboard, having run out of immediate ideas for dinner. As we love anything Thai or Indian, this seemed a rather good blend and has been made on many occasions since. The good news is that it can be served either hot or cold.

*Serves 4*                                              **GF WF DF V YF**

1 large onion, finely chopped
1 tablespoon cold pressed extra virgin olive oil
2 teaspoons ground cumin
1 teaspoon ground coriander
1 teaspoon mixed spice (pie spice)
A little minced chilli in oil or a chilli sauce*, optional
1 litre (4 cups) organic, pure tomato juice
3 teaspoons gluten-free vegetable bouillon powder (yeast- and dairy-free are
    available)
400ml (14fl oz) can reduced-fat coconut milk (Blue Dragon)
Salt and freshly ground black pepper (don't use salt on detox)
7g (¼oz) fresh coriander (cilantro) leaves, chopped

Cook the onion in the oil with all the spices and chilli until softened, over a fairly low heat so that the onion does not brown. Increase the heat to medium, and add the tomato juice and bouillon powder and stir occasionally while it is simmering. After about 20 minutes remove from the heat, stir in the coconut milk and leave to cool before puréeing in a blender until smooth.

• Reheat the soup over a medium heat for about 10 minutes, seasoning with salt, pepper and more chilli if necessary, and serve with a sprinkling of fresh coriander (cilantro). Alternatively, transfer the soup to a bowl, cool, cover and chill until needed.

## Beetroot and Cranberry Soup

Centuries ago, beetroot (beet) was grown for its leaves and not for the root. It was used to cure all sorts of ills. Most people throw away the leaves now, but they are a perfectly good substitute for spinach.

*Serves 6*                                                                    **GF WF DF V YF**

3 large fresh beetroots (beets), cooked in boiling water until tender, about 40
    minutes, or 2 x 200g (7oz) packets organic, cooked, whole beetroots (beets)
    (not in vinegar)
1 tablespoon cold pressed extra virgin olive oil
1 large onion, chopped
150g (5oz) cranberries, fresh or frozen, or 40g (⅓ cup) dried cranberries out of season
Pinch of ground cloves
Pinch of grated nutmeg
Pinch of cayenne pepper
Freshly ground black pepper
2 teaspoons of gluten-free vegetable bouillon powder (yeast- and dairy-free are
    available)
1 litre (4 cups) cranberry juice (Ocean Spray or similar)
Finely grated rind and juice of ½ an orange
6 teaspoons of half-fat crème fraîche for serving (don't use for dairy-free)
15g (½oz) chopped coriander (cilantro) leaves for serving

If using fresh beetroots (beets), top and tail them and peel them once they have cooled down. Discard the skins, stalks and the cooking liquid. Quarter either the fresh or the prepared beetroots (beets). Cook the beetroots (beets) and onion with the oil in a pan over medium heat for about 5 minutes. Stir frequently to prevent the vegetables sticking to the pan.

- Add the cranberries, spices, stock powder and cranberry juice, bring to the boil and then reduce the heat slightly so that it can simmer for about 30 minutes. When the onions are soft, remove the pan from the heat, add both the orange rind and juice and adjust the seasoning with the pepper.
- Once the soup is cool, purée until smooth in a blender, return to the pan and reheat. Serve hot with a spoonful of crème fraîche and a sprinkling of coriander (cilantro) in each bowl.

## Pasta and Bean Soup

We often have this soup as a meal in itself. It is a healthy, warming winter lunch or Sunday-night supper for all the family.

The Italians have all sorts of pastas which can be used for this dish, but it will be just as authentic if you use wheat-free macaroni, or you could break up some wheat-free tagliatelle.

*Serves 4–6*                                    **GF WF DF (V=optional) YF**

2 x 400g (14oz) cans borlotti beans or 450g (1lb) dried ones, soaked for
   12 hours
1 tablespoon cold pressed extra virgin olive oil and some extra for serving
85g/3oz chopped pancetta, or diced streaky, rindless smoked bacon (don't use on
   detox or vegetarian option)
1 large carrot, peeled and diced
1 onion, diced
2 celery stalks, diced
2 slim leeks, sliced
2 small red chillies (strength according to taste), chopped
1 teaspoon chopped rosemary
14 sage leaves, shredded
2 bay leaves
750ml (3 cups) or 1 bottle good-quality tomato pasta sauce
1 litre (4 cups) cold water (use some to rinse out the tomato sauce bottle)
1 tablespoon gluten-free vegetable bouillon powder (yeast- and dairy-free are
   available)
2 large garlic cloves, crushed
150g (1¾ cups) wheat-free pasta* (macaroni or small-sized pasta)
110g (1½ cups) French beans, cut into thirds
110g (¾ cup) frozen peas
Salt and freshly ground black pepper (don't use salt on detox)
15g (½oz) fresh parsley, chopped

If using canned beans, rinse them thoroughly and drain. If using dried beans, rinse them in cold water, then cook in unsalted boiling water for about 1½ hours until just soft.

- Heat the oil in a large heavy pan, add the pancetta or the bacon if you are using it, and cook for a few minutes until it turns golden. Then add the carrot, onion, celery, leeks, chillies and herbs. Alternatively, just heat the oil, add the vegetables, chillies and herbs.
- Continue to cook for about 3 minutes until the vegetables colour, then add the tomato sauce, water, bouillon powder and garlic, and cook for another 5 minutes.
- Stir in the borlotti beans and simmer for 30 minutes. Halfway through the cooking time, bring a pan of water to the boil and cook the pasta until al dente, drain and add to the soup.
- Meanwhile, cook the French beans and the peas together in boiling water until just cooked through, drain and add to the soup. Season to taste with salt and pepper, sprinkle with the parsley and serve piping hot with a swirl of olive oil.
- If the soup doesn't have enough liquid just add some more water or stock, as it is a very adaptable soup and can expand to suit a sudden influx of guests!

# Gingered Chicken Soup

Singles or couples could halve the quantities and enjoy this soup over several days. As with all chicken and stock dishes, allow it to get cold and then keep it chilled in the refrigerator until you need it. You can reboil the soup and add fresh bean sprouts, so it is a very good stand-by. You can also freeze this into portions and use for a quick lunch or appetizer.

A boiling chicken is the best thing for chicken soup, but they are increasingly hard to find. An ordinary roasting bird will be fine, but you must remove the meat after an hour or it will be too dry.

*Serves 10*                                                             **GF WF DF**

## Stock
1 boiling chicken, or an ordinary medium-sized roasting chicken,
    about 1.5kg (3lbs)
2 litres (8 cups) water plus 1 litre (4 cups) for topping up
Pinch of salt and 1 teaspoon black peppercorns (don't use salt on detox)
1 tablespoon cold pressed extra virgin olive oil
6cm (2in) piece root ginger, peeled and cut into chunks
1 large onion, coarsely chopped
2 tablespoons Thai fish sauce*

## Soup
6cm (2in) piece root ginger, peeled and grated
Pinch of salt (don't use salt on detox)
1 garlic clove, crushed
1 small chilli (hot or mild according to taste), finely chopped
300g (5 cups) bean sprouts
8 spring onions (scallions), finely chopped
15g (½oz) fresh coriander (cilantro) leaves, finely chopped
Soy sauce* to serve, optional

Put the chicken into a large pan and add the water, salt and peppercorns. Bring to the boil over a high heat. In a frying pan heat 1 tablespoon of oil and stir in the ginger and onion until they begin to colour slightly, and then add them to the chicken. When the water is boiling, add 1 tablespoon of the Thai fish sauce, turn the heat down and leave the chicken to simmer. Remove the chicken after an hour and, when it is cool enough, pick off the meat and shred it coarsely. Put the carcass back into the pot and simmer for another 2 hours.

- Strain the stock into a bowl and discard the carcass. When the stock is cold, cover and refrigerate it for at least 3 hours or overnight. You will then be able to skim off the layer of fat.

- You can make this stock 1 day in advance; just make sure the shredded chicken meat is kept in an airtight container in the fridge or it will become dry. When you want to make the soup, bring the stock to the boil and let it simmer, adding the shredded chicken, another table-spoon of fish sauce, the grated ginger, salt, garlic and chilli. Stir in the bean sprouts and cook for 1 minute.

- Serve the soup in warm bowls and top with the coriander (cilantro) and spring onions (scallions). As some people like to sprinkle their soup with soy sauce, serve it separately.

## chapter 20

# Salads

## Artichoke, Butter Bean and Fennel Salad

Although they have the flavour of globe artichokes, Jerusalem artichokes are in fact a relative of the sunflower. Jerusalem artichokes
appear in November and then throughout the winter. These artichokes
are warming and comforting, whereas artichoke hearts are light and
flowery, and so are ideal for the summer months.

*Serves 4*                                                    **GF WF DF V YF**

2 red onions, cut into 6
A little olive oil
Salt and freshly ground black pepper (don't use salt on detox)
A sprinkling of herbes de Provence (mixed herbs can be used as an alternative)
450g (1lb) Jerusalem artichokes, peeled or 400g (14oz) can artichoke hearts, or
    bottoms, drained, rinsed under cold water and halved
2 courgettes (zucchini), thickly sliced
400g (14oz) can butter (lima) beans, drained and rinsed under cold water
60g (2oz) prepared wild rocket (arugula)
1 large bulb fennel, outer layers removed, then trimmed and thinly sliced
15g (½oz) fresh basil leaves, shredded
Finely grated rind and juice of 1 lemon
Plenty of cold pressed extra virgin olive oil

Preheat the oven to 200°C/400°F/Gas Mark 6.

- Roast the onions in a baking tray with a drizzle of olive oil, a sprinkling of salt and pepper and herbes de Provence until they are dark brown at the edges and soft in the centre.
- Put a pan of water on to boil. Drop the Jerusalem artichokes into the water and simmer for about 15 minutes, depending on their size. Drain and leave to cool.
- Meanwhile, cook the courgette (zucchini) in another pan of boiling water until al dente, then allow to cool.
- Mix the butter (lima) beans and rocket (arugula) with the fennel and basil leaves in a big salad bowl. Add the artichoke hearts if you are using them, or the cooled Jerusalem artichokes and the red onions and courgettes (zucchini). Season to taste with salt and freshly ground black pepper, the grated rind and lemon juice and, finally, the extra virgin olive oil.
- Toss the salad and serve straightaway with fresh wheat-free bread rolls*, a baked potato or a potato salad as a main course.

## Asparagus Salad with Coriander and Ginger Dressing

This salad is made up of a delicious combination of vegetables, but you can always make another kind of salad – for example, a prawn (shrimp) or chicken and avocado salad – and just use this delicious dressing recipe.

*Serves 4*                                              **GF WF DF V YF**

2 large red onions, cut into 10
Cold pressed extra virgin olive oil
1 teaspoon fresh thyme leaves
200g (7oz) pack prepared fresh asparagus tips
3 medium courgettes (zucchini)

**Dressing**
Juice of 1 lemon
1 teaspoon Dijon mustard*
1 tablespoon clear honey
4 tablespoons bottled fat-free French dressing or cold pressed extra virgin olive oil
  for yeast-free diet
1 teaspoon coriander seeds
2 teaspoons finely grated root ginger
Salt and freshly ground black pepper (don't use salt on detox)
20g (¾oz) chopped fresh parsley

Preheat the oven to 200°C/400°F/Gas Mark 6.
- Put the onions into a baking tray, drizzle with oil and sprinkle with thyme. Bake them for 20–30 minutes, until blackened at the edges but soft in the centre.
- Meanwhile, cook the asparagus in boiling water until just tender. Drain and refresh them under cold running water.
- Cut each courgette (zucchini) into about 10 diagonal chunks and cook in a pan of boiling water until just cooked through but still slightly crunchy. Drain and refresh under cold running water.
- Arrange the hot onions and both the vegetables on a serving dish. Now make the dressing by whisking all the ingredients together (except the parsley) in a bowl in the given order. Pour the dressing all over the salad, sprinkle with parsley and serve or cover and chill until needed.

# Super Summer Mixed Salad

Ensure you use fresh and crisp ingredients for the salad as these provide the maximum nutrients as well as the best flavours and textures.

*Serves 1*                                                    **GF WF DF V YF**

### Salad
80g (½ cup) grated raw beetroot (beet)
40g (⅓ cup) finely sliced radishes
30g (½ cup) finely sliced celery
40g (½ cup) finely shredded cabbage leaves
20g (¾oz) trimmed watercress
60g (1 cup) sprouts – use any kind or combination: alfalfa, bean sprouts, mung,
  chickpeas (garbanzos), lentils
40g (½ cup) grated carrots
1 thinly sliced vine tomato
50g (⅓ cup) thinly sliced cucumber

### Dressing
Dash of cold pressed extra virgin olive oil
Little fresh lemon or lime juice
½ small garlic clove, crushed (optional and according to taste)
Little minced chilli in oil or freshly chopped chilli (optional and according to taste)
Freshly ground black pepper

Combine all the prepared salad ingredients in a bowl. Toss in the oil and lemon or lime juice according to preference, then toss in the garlic and chilli if you are using them. Season according to taste and serve immediately for ultimate freshness.

## Vegetable Kebabs with Walnut and Rice Salad

There is absolutely no reason why kebabs should contain meat, so here are some which will be ideal if you have vegetarian guests or just want a lower fat and more easily digestible feast. You can cook the rice the day before and keep it covered and chilled until needed.

*Serves 4*                                                    **GF WF DF V YF**

2 heaped teaspoons fresh thyme leaves
1 large garlic clove, crushed
Light sprinkling dried chilli flakes, or minced chillies in oil
4 tablespoons cold pressed extra virgin olive oil
Salt and freshly ground black pepper (don't use salt on detox)
2 cobs sweetcorn, each cut into 4
1 courgette (zucchini), cut into 8
3 large flat mushrooms, peeled and stalk removed (don't use if yeast sensitive,
    replace with another vegetable)
1 green and 1 red pepper (bell pepper), seeded and cut into squares
8 fresh bay leaves
2 small red onions, cut into 8

### Yogurt dip
400ml (1¾ cups) virtually fat-free set natural (plain) sheep, goat or soy yogurt
1 small garlic clove, crushed
7g (¼oz) chopped fresh mint leaves
7g (¼oz) chopped fresh flat-leaf parsley leaves

**Rice salad**

170g/1 cup wild rice, cooked until tender then drained

170g/1 cup brown rice, cooked until tender then drained

60g (½ cup) chopped walnuts (don't use on weeks 2 and 3 of the detox)

60g (½ cup) halved almonds

60g (⅔ cup) plump raisins

3 spring onions (scallions), chopped

7g (¼oz) each chopped mint, chives and parsley

Grated rind and juice of 1 orange

2 tablespoons cold pressed extra virgin olive oil

Minced chilli in oil

8 bamboo skewers, soaked in water for 5 minutes

First prepare the vegetable kebabs. Mix the thyme, garlic and chillies in a bowl with the olive oil and seasoning, and reserve. Cook the sweetcorn in boiling water for 10 minutes. Lift them out and leave to drain. Blanch the courgette (zucchini) in boiling water for 3 minutes. Drain, refresh under cold running water and set aside.

- Blanch the mushrooms in boiling water for 1 minute. Drain, refresh under cold running water and set aside. When they are cool enough to touch, cut into quarters.
- Thread all the vegetables and a bay leaf on to each of the skewers. Brush with the garlic oil and cook for 10 minutes under a very hot grill (broiler). Turn them over, brush with the remaining sauce and cook for a further 10 minutes, or until the onions and peppers (bell peppers) are cooked through.
- While the vegetables are cooking, make the yogurt dip. Combine all the ingredients in a bowl and season according to taste with salt and pepper. Alternatively, make this in advance and cover and chill until needed.
- Quickly put the rice salad together by combining all the ingredients in the given order in a bowl and season to taste with salt and pepper.
- Transfer the rice salad on to a large serving dish. Arrange the cooked kebabs over the rice and serve immediately accompanied by the dip.

## Chicken Liver and Cranberry Terrine with Broccoli and Almond Salad

One of my favourite activities in France is, I am sure you will not be surprised to hear, eating in restaurants. At lunchtime, I browse through the menu and hum and ha over the delicious choices, but often succumb to the most traditional terrine, which I know will always be perfect. This is my current favourite. It freezes well, so I make it all the time.

*Serves 10*                                                              **GF WF DF**

### Terrine
300g (10½oz) rindless, smoked streaky bacon rashers (slices)
400g (14oz) chicken livers, rinsed under cold running water and drained
500g (1lb 2oz) extra-lean minced (ground) pork
1 onion, finely chopped
2 extra large garlic cloves, crushed
2 tablespoons chopped fresh parsley
1 tablespoon fresh thyme leaves or 1 teaspoon dried thyme
2 tablespoons brandy
75g (⅔ cup) dried cranberries, or 110g (4oz) fresh or frozen cranberries (defrosted)
Salt and freshly ground black pepper (don't use salt on detox)
3 bay leaves

### Broccoli and almond salad
565g (1¼lbs) prepared broccoli florets
285g (10oz) mini vine tomatoes, halved
1 bulb fennel, trimmed, all tough layers removed and then finely sliced
About ½ a bottle of virtually fat-free French dressing (as much as you need to toss the salad) or cold pressed extra virgin olive oil
110g (¾ cup) whole almonds with their skins, halved
15g (½oz) chopped fresh flat-leaf parsley

1kg (2lb) loaf tin (pan)

Preheat the oven to 180°C/350°F/Gas Mark 4.

- First make the terrine. Stretch most of the bacon across the base and up the sides of the loaf tin (pan), allowing the ends to hang over the edges. Place the remaining bacon in a food processor together with the livers, pork and onion, and chop finely but do not purée.
- Turn the mixture into a bowl and mix in the garlic, herbs, brandy and cranberries and season with salt and pepper. Spoon the mixture into the prepared loaf tin (pan). Smooth the top of the mixture to the edges, lay the bay leaves on top and fold in the ends of the bacon.
- Cover with foil and stand in a roasting pan that is two-thirds filled with cold water. Cook in the oven for 2 hours, until the juices run clear when the middle of the loaf is pierced with a skewer. Remove the foil and cover with greaseproof (waxed) paper.
- Cover with a treble layer of foil, put a weight on top and leave it to cool, standing on a tray in case any juices escape. It should then be left to chill overnight.
- Now make the broccoli and almond salad. Cook the broccoli in a pan of boiling water for 3 minutes, drain and refresh under cold running water. Transfer to a salad bowl, mix in the tomatoes and fennel, and sprinkle liberally with the dressing, almonds, salt, pepper and parsley.
- Turn the terrine out on to a serving plate; serve with the broccoli and almond salad. A big green salad – spinach, rocket (arugula), chicory, salad leaves, cucumber and other favourites – lightly tossed in cold pressed extra virgin olive oil and black pepper is also a delicious accompaniment.

## Sesame Salmon Fingers with Sugar Snap Salad

The good thing about salmon is that it is so filling, whether it is served hot or cold. I often make this dish for dinner for two and then invite a friend to lunch the next day, serving what is left as a delicious cold dish.

*Serves 4*                                                                   **GF WF DF YF**

### Salad
250g (9oz) dwarf green beans, top and tailed
350g (12oz) fresh asparagus, cut into 15cm (6in) lengths
200g (7oz) prepared sugar snap peas
225g (8oz) pack sunblush tomatoes in olive oil, coarsely chopped
2 tablespoons lemon juice
15g (½oz) chives, chopped

### Fish fingers
450g (1lb) salmon fillet, skinned and cut into 4 equal strips to look like thick fingers
2 heaped tablespoons wheat-free flour* spread over a dinner plate, seasoned with
    salt and freshly ground black pepper (don't use salt on detox)
2 large free-range eggs, beaten in a wide bowl
About 110g (4oz) sesame seeds, more or less as you want, spread over a dinner plate
2 tablespoons cold pressed extra virgin olive oil
1 lemon and 1 lime, quartered for decoration and serving

Make the salad first. Bring a big pan of water to the boil, add the beans and asparagus, and cook for 3 minutes. Then add the sugar snap peas and cook for a further 3 minutes. Lift all the vegetables out with a slotted spoon, drain and refresh them under cold running water and set aside on a plate. Leave them to cool down while you prepare the fish fingers.

• Pat the salmon dry with absorbent kitchen paper, roll it in the plate of seasoned flour, dip the salmon into the eggs and finally into the plate of sesame seeds. You can sprinkle more seeds over the fish if you like.

• Toss the salad vegetables with the chopped tomatoes in their oil, lemon juice and chives and season with salt and pepper. Arrange the salad over a flat serving dish.

• Now briefly heat the oil in a non-stick frying pan (skillet) over a high heat and fry the salmon fingers for about 2–3 minutes on each side, until the seeds are golden and the outer layers of fish are opaque. Lift the salmon fingers out and on to a plate covered with quadruple folded absorbent kitchen paper.

• After a minute or two, arrange the salmon fingers diagonally across the salad, decorate with the wedges of lemon or lime and serve immediately. Squeeze either lemon or lime juice over your salmon and enjoy it while it is hot.

## Prawn, Mango and Cucumber Salad

You can choose the type of prawns (shrimp) to suit your budget. Dill adds a mild aniseed tang, which contrasts well with the mango and cucumber. Radishes lose their pungency once cut, so prepare them at the last minute. The lime juice will enhance the sweetness of the radishes.

*Serves 4*                                                        **GF WF DF YF**

### Dressing
Juice of 1 lime
1 teaspoon Dijon mustard*
1 tablespoon clear honey
3 tablespoons bottled fat-free French dressing or cold pressed extra virgin olive oil for yeast-free diets
Salt and freshly ground black pepper (don't use salt on detox)

### Salad
1 ripe mango, peeled and stoned (pitted)
¾ cucumber, peeled
1 large bunch fresh radishes, trimmed
450g (16oz) large king prawns (jumbo shrimp), peeled, heads and tails removed
15g (½oz) fresh dill, finely chopped

First make the dressing: whisk together the lime juice, mustard, honey, French dressing or oil and season to taste.

• Now make the salad. Cut the mango flesh into small chunks and thinly slice the cucumber. Arrange the cucumber slices in a ring on a large serving plate. Finely slice the radishes and combine them in a bowl with the prawns (shrimp) and mango chunks. Arrange this mixture in the centre and spoon over the dressing. Sprinkle with dill and serve immediately or keep chilled until needed.

## chapter 21

# Vegetable and Vegetarian Dishes

## Winter Thai Stir-Fry

As you would if making a fresh salad, plan ahead to make sure that you have fresh and crisp ingredients for the stir-fry to ensure that you get the maximum nutrients as well as the best flavours and textures.

*Serves 1*                                                                    **GF WF DF**

70g (1 cup) thinly sliced red cabbage

60g (½ cup) thinly cut carrot sticks

60g (¾ cup) small broccoli florets

60g (¾ cup) small cauliflower florets

60g (1 cup) mung or bean sprouts (or any other fresh vegetables you have available)

1 tablespoon cold pressed extra virgin olive oil

½ garlic clove, crushed

½ small chilli (any strength), finely chopped, remove seeds for a milder taste

¼ teaspoon coriander seeds

1 heaped teaspoon grated root ginger

1 tablespoon organic soy sauce*

Salt and freshly ground black pepper (don't use salt on detox)

1 tablespoon chopped fresh coriander (cilantro) leaves

First, prepare all your vegetables. Heat the oil in the wok over a high heat.

- Stir-fry the cabbage, carrots, broccoli, cauliflower and the remaining cup of your choice of vegetables together for 3 minutes. If your choice is bean sprouts or some other very fine vegetable, add them after 3 minutes along with the garlic, chilli, coriander seeds and ginger. Fry everything together for about another 2 minutes by which time the bean sprouts will be cooked through too.
- Toss the ingredients regularly to ensure that they cook evenly. Season with the soy sauce and pepper, sprinkle with the coriander (cilantro) leaves and serve immediately.

## Tomato and Pesto Tarts

These very cute little tarts are ideal for picnics and lunches al fresco. They can also be served as a perfect appetizer at parties. However, you do need the more expensive vine tomatoes because their taste is so superior, and this always matters in simple recipes.

*Serves 8–9*                                                                                        **GF WF V YF**

**Pastry**
200g (1¾ cups) wheat-free flour*
125g (4½oz) dairy-free margarine or butter, cut into 8 pieces
Pinch of salt (don't use salt on detox)
1 medium free-range egg
A little cold water

**Filling**
9 medium-sized, vine-ripe tomatoes, stalks removed, and each one scratched with
    a sharp knife and immersed in a bowl of boiling water for 5 minutes or until the
    skins peel off with ease
120g (4oz tub) fresh deli-made pesto or a bottled organic pesto
Freshly ground black pepper
About 60g (2oz) pecorino cheese shavings (or other sheep's cheese)
Pinch of cayenne pepper
Basil leaves to decorate, optional

3 x 6-cup mini tart trays

Preheat the oven to 180°C/350°F/Gas Mark 4. Make the pastry in a food processor. Put all the pastry ingredients, except the water, in the processor and whizz for a few seconds until the mixture resembles breadcrumbs. Cautiously add the water and process briefly until it comes together into a ball of dough.

- Remove the dough, wrap it in clingfilm (plastic wrap) and freeze for 10 minutes. Meanwhile peel off the tomato skins, cut the tops off and discard.
- Roll out the dough into a medium–thick pastry on a floured board and then cut into 18 circles. Line the cups of the baking tray with the pastry circles and prick the bases with a fork.
- Quarter each tomato, removing the white core and attached seeds, which you can discard. Place a double thickness of absorbent kitchen paper on a clean surface and lay the tomatoes on top. Cover with another double layer, which will soak up the excess juices. Slice the tomatoes into smaller pieces that you can arrange nicely in each pastry case. Divide the tomatoes between the pastry cases and season them with a little black pepper. Spoon about a teaspoon of the pesto over the top of each tomato filled tart, then sprinkle with pecorino shavings and cayenne pepper.
- Bake them in the oven for 25 minutes or until the pastry is golden and the filling is bubbling.
- Let the tarts cool down and when they are just cool enough to handle you will be able to lift them out of the tray. Serve the tarts straight-away, two on each plate and decorate with some basil leaves.

## Vegetable Spring Rolls

These spring rolls are uncooked and therefore easy to make, as well as being healthy. You can either serve them as an appetizer, or as a main course with a bowl of steamed fragrant Thai rice. The rice wrappers are available from large supermarkets or Chinese grocery stores.

*Serves 4*                                                                **GF WF DF V**

### Spring rolls
1 small red pepper (bell pepper), seeded and cut into very fine julienne strips
Drizzle of cold pressed extra virgin olive oil
110g (4oz) bean sprouts, blanched for 1 minute in boiling water, drained and
    refreshed under cold running water
¼ small cucumber, peeled, seeded and cut into fine julienne strips
1 medium carrot, peeled and cut into fine julienne strips
2 spring onions (scallions), cut into very fine strips
7g (¼oz) each mint, coriander (cilantro) and basil leaves, coarsely chopped
60g (⅓ cup) roasted, salted almonds, crushed
Freshly ground black pepper
2 packets rice wrappers (12)

### Dipping sauce
Juice of 2 limes
2 tablespoons soy sauce*
4 teaspoons rice or sherry vinegar
Minced chilli in oil or dried flaked chillies
2 tablespoons clear runny honey
3 teaspoons sesame seeds
4 tablespoons tomato ketchup

First make the rolls. Stir-fry the peppers in the oil in a pan for a few minutes and leave to cool. Mix the peppers with the bean sprouts, cucumber, carrot, spring onions (scallions), herbs and nuts in a bowl. Season with pepper but not salt, as you are already using salted almonds.

• Dip a rice wrapper in warm water until it is pliable and then place on a very wet tea towel on a clean surface. Generously pile a line of the vegetable mixture along the lower edge. Roll the rice wrapper away from you, tucking in the ends as you go. If you dip your fingers in water this prevents the rolls from getting sticky.

- Place each roll seam-side down on a serving plate, and make up each roll in the same way.
- To make the dipping sauce, mix the ingredients together in a small saucepan, bring to the boil and boil the sauce for about 30 seconds. Drizzle it all over the plate of spring rolls or serve alongside.
- You can decorate this dish with some exotic flower heads or leaves and serve immediately.

## Broad Beans on Lemon Crostini

You may think it is such a bore to peel the beans but it really is worth it, not only are they sweet and tender but they are a lovely, cheerful bright green. This dish is ideal for lunch al fresco, or as an appetizer.

*Serves 2*                                                          **GF WF DF V**

250g (9oz) frozen or fresh baby broad (fava) beans
2 garlic cloves, crushed
Salt and freshly ground black pepper (don't use salt on detox)
2 tablespoons cold pressed extra virgin olive oil, plus plenty extra for sprinkling
7g (¼oz) coarsely chopped flat-leaf parsley
15g (½oz) fresh basil leaves, shredded
2 white wheat-free bread rolls*, refreshed according to instructions on the packet,
   tops sliced off and discarded or 1 small wheat-free baguette*, refreshed
   according to the instructions on the packet, and then halved horizontally
Juice of ½ a lemon

Cook the broad (fava) beans in boiling water for about 3 minutes and drain. Once they are cool enough to handle, pop them from their skins. Discard the skins and put the beans into a small pan.

- Add the garlic, salt and pepper and the 2 tablespoons of olive oil. Gently stew the beans for about 5 minutes, add the herbs and cook for another 3 minutes.
- Place the prepared bread on to two plates and spoon the beans and oil over each one. Squeeze over the lemon juice, drizzle with plenty of extra virgin olive oil, so that the bread absorbs it, and then sprinkle with pepper and serve.

## Leeks Napolitano

In the grim days of February, I remind my parents how satisfying it is for them to battle against the bitter, freezing north Norfolk wind, and venture down to the kitchen garden, to dig up a bundle of sturdy leeks for our lunch! Very conveniently, I cannot possibly dig them up myself, with such a bad back, but I can cook a delicious lunch using them!

*Serves 3 (make double the quantity for 6)*                    **GF WF DF V YF**

1 onion, finely chopped
1 teaspoon dried thyme leaves
1 teaspoon dried herbes de Provence (mixed herbs can be used as an alternative)
1 tablespoon cold pressed extra virgin olive oil plus extra for sprinkling
400g/14oz can organic chopped tomatoes
1 teaspoon gluten-free vegetable bouillon powder (yeast- and dairy-free is available)
Salt and freshly ground black pepper (don't use salt on detox)
7g (¼oz) flat-leaf parsley, finely chopped
500g (1lb 2oz) prepared leeks
Sprinkling of cayenne pepper

Preheat the oven to 180°C/350°F/Gas Mark 4.
- Cook the onion and herbs in a pan with the tablespoon of oil until nearly soft but not browned. Stir in the tomatoes, bouillon powder and pepper. Simmer for another 20 minutes or until completely soft. Remove from the heat and stir in the parsley.
- Cut each leek into 3 pieces and plunge into a pan of boiling water to cook for 5 minutes. Drain and refresh under cold water. Transfer the leeks to an ovenproof serving dish, arranging them neatly.
- Spoon the tomato sauce all over the leeks and sprinkle with a little oil and cayenne pepper. Bake in the oven for about 25 minutes until the leeks are soft.

# Griddled Sweet Potatoes with Three-Bean Salad

This recipe is a good filling and warming winter dish that is ideal for lunch, a light supper or as an appetizer. You can use any of your favourite beans and mix and match your own combinations.

*Serves 3*                                                      **GF WF DF V YF**

### Potatoes
600g (1lb 5oz) sweet potatoes (orange flesh), peeled and cut into 1.2 cm/½in thick slices
1 tablespoon cold pressed extra virgin olive oil

### Bean salad
150g (scant 1 cup) canned red kidney beans, drained and rinsed under cold water
150g (¾ cup) canned butter (lima) beans, drained and rinsed under cold water
150g (scant 2 cups) fine green beans, cut into thirds
Drizzle of bottled fat-free French dressing, or cold pressed extra virgin olive oil if yeast-free
Freshly ground black pepper
Sprinkling of chopped fresh parsley

Bring a pan of water to the boil and then cook the potatoes for 5 minutes. Carefully lift them out with a slotted spoon or spatula and leave to drain. Heat the oil in a frying pan (skillet) over a high heat for a few seconds and then place the potato slices carefully in the pan. Season with a little pepper and sauté the potatoes until they are dark brown at the edges, golden in the middle and soft all the way through.

- Meanwhile, make the salad. Rinse the kidney beans and butter (lima) beans under cold water and drain them. Bring a saucepan of water to the boil; add the green beans and cook them for 2 minutes so that they remain crunchy. Add the kidney beans and the butter (lima) beans, to the pan and cook for 1 minute more. Drain all the beans in a colander, rinse them with warm water and drain again.
- Put all the beans into a salad bowl, toss them in the dressing, season to taste with pepper and sprinkle with the fresh parsley. Serve the sauté potato slices in an overlapping circle in the centre of each plate, top with a mound of the bean salad and eat straightaway.

## Feta, Courgette and Tomato Pizza

Here are two easy ways to conjure up a pizza: one is instant while the other takes a fraction more time but is, of course, fresher and even more delicious. You can put any topping you like on to this pizza base, and be as extravagant (artichokes, asparagus, prawns or shrimp) or as economical (cheese and tomato) as you like. I find that half a pizza is enough for me, so we usually share one. If you are on your own, I suggest halving the pizza and freezing it for another time. Simply defrost it as usual and cook until piping hot. (Do not do this with seafood pizzas).

*Serves 1*                                                          **GF WF V YF**

### Instant pizza

400g (14oz) can ratatouille – high quality brand will ensure lots of courgettes
    (zucchini)
1 small garlic clove, crushed
2 tablespoons tomato purée (paste)
Salt and freshly ground black pepper (don't use salt on detox)
Minced chilli in oil or freshly chopped chilli, according to taste
1 ready-made wheat-free pizza base* (see stockists list page 258)
110g (4oz) feta cheese, thinly sliced
Large pinch of herbes de Provence (mixed herbs can be used as an alternative)
Drizzle of cold pressed extra virgin olive oil

### Super pizza

240g (8½oz) sunblush tomatoes in olive oil, (available in Sainsbury's) drained,
    but keep the oil for later
1 small garlic clove, crushed
2 tablespoons tomato purée (paste)
Salt and freshly ground black pepper (don't use salt on detox)
Minced chilli or freshly chopped chilli, according to taste
1 ready-made wheat-free pizza base* (see stockists list page 258)
1 small courgette (zucchini), finely sliced
110g (4oz) feta cheese, thinly sliced
A large pinch of herbes de Provence (or mixed herbs)

Preheat the oven to 220°C/425°F/Gas Mark 7.

- To make the instant pizza, mix the ratatouille in a bowl with the garlic, tomato purée (paste), salt and pepper and chilli seasoning; spread the mixture over the pizza base and slide it on to a baking tray. Cover with the feta cheese, sprinkle liberally with the herbs and some more black pepper and drizzle with oil. Bake for 25 minutes or until bubbling and very hot.

- To make the super pizza, mix the sunblush tomatoes in a bowl with the garlic, tomato purée (paste), salt and pepper and chilli seasoning; spread the mixture evenly over the pizza base, pressing it right to the edges. Slide it on to a baking tray.

- Bring a pan of water to the boil and cook the courgettes (zucchini) for about 3 minutes or until they are just cooked but still crunchy. Drain and rinse under cold running water. Pat them dry in a double thickness of absorbent kitchen paper and then arrange the courgettes (zucchini) all over the pizza. Cover with the feta cheese, sprinkle liberally with the herbs and some more black pepper, and drizzle with some of the sunblush tomato oil. Bake for 25 minutes or until bubbling and very hot.

## Lemon and Spinach Risotto

Cheap and easy recipes are indispensable, whether feeding the family or entertaining. This risotto is ideal for either scenario, and can be served with a big green and herb salad and a tomato and basil salad.

*Serves 4*                                    **GF WF V YF DF (optional)**

75g (¼ cup) dairy-free margarine or butter
1 tablespoon cold pressed extra virgin olive oil
1 onion, finely chopped
300g (1½ cups) Arborio rice
1 litre (4 cups) vegetable stock or 2 teaspoons gluten-free vegetable bouillon
    powder (yeast- and dairy-free are available) dissolved in boiling water
125g (4½oz) fresh young spinach leaves, coarsely chopped
Finely grated rind and juice of 1 lemon
60g (½ cup) freshly grated reduced-fat hard cheese or dairy-free cheese
Salt and freshly ground black pepper (don't use salt on detox)

Melt the margarine or butter with the oil in a large pan over a low heat and stir in the onions. Cook them until soft but do not let them brown. Add the rice, stir for about 30 seconds and then pour in the vegetable stock. Simmer the rice until it is plump and soft, stirring regularly, adding more stock if needed.

- Gently stir in the spinach, simmer for another couple of minutes until it has softened, and then stir in the lemon rind and juice, cheese, salt and pepper.
- Serve the risotto immediately. If you want to reheat the risotto the next day, add some more stock, lemon juice and a dash of oil and heat very gently, stirring constantly.

## Sweet Red Pepper Dip

Suitably pink for St Valentine's Day, this dip can be as extravagant or as simple as you like. For the best effect, serve the dip in a glass bowl in the middle of a large glass dish, surrounded by your chosen dippers. You can dip cooked king prawns (jumbo shrimp) or voluptuous barely cooked scallops, lightly cooked asparagus tips or grilled baby courgettes (zucchini). The leftover dip is delicious for lunch the next day.

*Serves 4*                                                    **GF WF V DF (optional)**

3 red peppers (bell peppers), seeded and coarsely chopped
1 red onion, coarsely chopped
1 teaspoon fresh thyme leaves
1 garlic clove, crushed
1 tablespoon cold pressed extra virgin olive oil
1 tablespoon balsamic vinegar
Salt and freshly ground black pepper (don't use salt on detox)
1 finely chopped chilli (choose your own preferred strength)
125ml (½ cup) 50% reduced-fat crème fraîche, chilled or dairy-free natural (plain)
   set yogurt

**To serve**
450g (1lb) fresh asparagus, lightly cooked in boiling water until
   al dente, drained, refreshed under cold running water
Or, less expensively, 1 packet organic yellow 100% corn chips

Cook the peppers and onions in a saucepan over a medium heat with the thyme, garlic and oil for about 10 minutes, stirring occasionally. Add the balsamic vinegar, salt, pepper and chilli and continue to cook for another 15 minutes until they are browned, soft and mushy.

- Leave the mixture to cool and then purée in a blender. Transfer the mixture to a bowl and when it is cold, stir in the crème fraîche and adjust the seasoning to taste.
- Spoon the dip into a bowl, cover and chill until needed. Serve it with the asparagus or corn chips.

## Fusilli with Roasted Vegetables and Olives

This easy pasta dish can be served hot or cold, and you can use any seasonal vegetables you like as long as they roast well. Other ideas are to use chopped aubergine (eggplant), French beans, squashes or baby carrots.

*Serves 4–6*                                   **GF WF DF V YF**

1 yellow pepper (bell pepper) and 1 green pepper (bell pepper), seeded and
   chopped into large pieces
2 small red onions, cut into 8 wedges
3 courgettes (zucchini), cut into about 8–10 diagonal chunks
4 vine tomatoes, stalks and tops removed
110–140g (4–5oz) asparagus tips
5 tablespoons cold pressed extra virgin olive oil and 2 tablespoons extra virgin olive
   oil for tossing the pasta
1 heaped tablespoon chopped fresh rosemary leaves
250g (3 cups) wheat-free fusilli pasta*
Salt and freshly ground black pepper (don't use salt on detox)
1 large garlic clove, crushed
85g (½cup) stoned (pitted) black olives*
Minced chilli in oil, fresh chilli or chilli sauce*, optional
7g (¼oz) fresh flat-leaf parsley, finely chopped

Preheat the oven to 200°C/400°F/Gas Mark 6.

- Place all the vegetables in the oven's roasting tray or a big roasting pan, and sprinkle with the 5 tablespoons of olive oil. Make sure everything is evenly coated, and then sprinkle over all the rosemary. Roast the vegetables in the oven for about 40 minutes until all the vegetables are cooked – some will be browned or crispy at the edges and some will just be softly cooked and glazed. I usually turn the tray around for more even baking but if you have a fan oven this shouldn't be necessary.
- About halfway through the cooking time, bring a pan of water to the boil and add some salt. Cook the pasta according to the instructions until al dente. Drain the pasta, transfer to a serving bowl and toss in the 2 tablespoons of extra virgin olive oil. Season with salt, pepper, garlic, mix in the olives and add the chilli if you like your pasta spiced up.
- As soon as the vegetables are ready, mix them into the pasta, sprinkle with fresh parsley and serve hot.
- Alternatively, wait for the mixture to cool, cover and chill until needed, but serve at room temperature.

## Cheese Roulade with Walnuts

This is a brilliant vegetarian alternative to the roast meats, game or turkey that we usually cook during the Easter and Christmas periods, and will ensure that no vegetarians feel left out of the festivities.

This roulade works well when made the day before. Not only does it cut more easily, it also gives you more time to pamper yourself before friends or family arrive!

*Serves 6*                                                                **GF WF V YF**

**Roulade**

30g (2 tablespoons) dairy-free margarine or butter
30g (¼ cup) wheat-free flour*
200ml (¾ cup) skimmed milk
Salt and freshly ground black pepper (don't use salt on detox)
Freshly grated nutmeg
Pinch of cayenne pepper
4 large free-range eggs, separated
1 tablespoon of Dijon mustard*
85g (¾ cup) grated reduced-fat hard cheese
60g (½ cup) walnuts, very finely chopped, plus the same amount again for
    sprinkling on the non-stick paper

**Filling**

500g (2 cups) virtually fat-free fromage frais
425g (15oz can) artichoke hearts, well drained and thinly sliced
7g (¼oz) chopped fresh parsley


33 x 23cm (13 x 9in) Swiss-roll/roulade tin (pan), lined with non-stick baking paper
A large sheet of non-stick paper sprinkled with 60g (½ cup) chopped walnuts,
    ready to turn the cooked roulade out immediately it comes out of the oven

Preheat the oven to 200°C/400°F/Gas Mark 6.

- Melt the margarine or butter in a small saucepan, stir in the flour and cook for a minute before gradually incorporating the milk. Let the mixture come to the boil, stirring all the time and cook for a couple of minutes. Remove it from the heat and season with salt, pepper, nutmeg and cayenne. Stir in the egg yolks, mustard, grated cheese and 60g (½ cup) of walnuts.

- In a large bowl, whisk the egg whites until stiff and then fold them into the cheese mixture. Gently pour and scrape the mixture into the prepared tin (pan) and bake in the oven for about 10–15 minutes, or until golden and firm to touch.

- Sprinkle a sheet of non-stick baking paper with the remaining 60g (½ cup) walnuts and turn the roulade out on to it. The easiest way to do this is by flipping the roulade tin (pan) down on to the paper. Quickly peel the lining paper off the roulade and discard it. Cover with a clean cloth and leave to cool.

- When cool, lift the cloth off the roulade and spread the roulade with the fromage frais. Now arrange the artichokes over the fromage frais, and sprinkle the parsley over the artichokes, season with a little salt and plenty of pepper and roll up the roulade. Using the paper to help you, pull the roulade over a little at a time until it is completely rolled up. Keep it wrapped up securely in the paper and chill until needed.

- Trim off the edges and serve the roulade cut into slices as an apperteizer or serve whole and nicely decorated for a main course.

## Asparagus and Spinach Picnic Tart

If you have a vegetable patch in your garden, you will probably agree that, amongst the plants which are classed as 'stalks and shoots', the undoubted aristocrat and noblest of them all is the asparagus. Its short season means that there is no time to get tired of this epicurean vegetable. This recipe makes a few stems go a long way.

*Serves 6*                                                    **GF WF V YF**

### Pastry
250g (2¼ cups) wheat-free flour*
125g (4½oz) dairy-free margarine or butter, cut into 8 pieces
1 large free-range egg
Pinch of salt (don't use salt on detox)
A little cold water

### Filling
1 bundle asparagus, about 19 long spears, trimmed to fit into the pastry-lined
    baking tray
125g (4½oz) fresh young spinach leaves, washed
250ml (1 cup) reduced-fat crème fraîche
85g (¾ cup) grated reduced-fat hard cheese or vegetarian cheese
4 large free-range eggs, lightly beaten in a bowl
Freshly grated nutmeg
Salt and freshly ground black pepper (don't use salt on detox)
Pinch of cayenne pepper

A 24cm (9½in) square, loose-bottomed non-stick baking tray, lined with a square
    of non-stick baking paper (you will also need a second piece) and ceramic baking
    beans for baking blind

Preheat the oven to 200°C/400°F/Gas Mark 6.

- Make the pastry by briefly blending all the ingredients, except the water, in a food processor until it resembles breadcrumbs. Now add a little water and whizz briefly until the pastry comes together into a ball of dough. Remove the pastry, wrap it in clingfilm (plastic wrap) and freeze for 10 minutes.
- Plunge the asparagus into a pan of boiling water, lift out after a minute, drain and refresh under cold running water. Now, plunge the spinach leaves into the same boiling water for a minute, lift out, drain and refresh under cold running water.
- Roll out the pastry on a floured board, lift it over the baking tray and carefully line it, cutting the edges with a sharp knife. Prick the pastry base with a fork, line with the paper and ceramic baking beans and bake blind for 10 minutes.
- Remove the paper and ceramic beans and bake for a further 5 minutes to cook the base a little more.
- Cover the pastry base with the spinach leaves. Mix the crème fraîche and the hard cheese into the beaten eggs and season with a sprinkling of nutmeg, salt and pepper.
- Pour the mixture over the spinach, then arrange all the asparagus in a line from one end to the other. Sprinkle with cayenne pepper if desired and bake in the oven for about 30 minutes, or until the pastry is golden and the filling set.
- Serve warm with a big mixed herb salad or leave to cool and then chill until needed.

## Mushroom and Mozzarella Lasagne

If you use ripe vine tomatoes, the sauce should be light, sweet and full of flavour, which will contrast beautifully with the rich, deep, intense flavour of the mushrooms. You can go mad and use double or treble the amount of dried wild mushrooms, and you can use wild fresh mushrooms in place of the cultivated ones – pure magic!

*Serves 6*                                                                           **GF WF V**

### Tomato sauce
2 large onions, finely chopped
2 tablespoons cold pressed extra virgin olive oil
1.5kg (3½lbs) fresh ripe vine or plum tomatoes, peeled, quartered and cores and
    seeds removed (to remove skins, submerge tomatoes in a bowl of boiling water,
    slash the skins and they will start to loosen. Remove with a sharp knife)
Salt and freshly ground black pepper (don't use salt on detox)
2 large garlic cloves, crushed
Minced chilli in oil (according to taste)
2 bay leaves
2 heaped teaspoons fresh thyme leaves
2 heaped tablespoons sun-dried tomato sauce

### Mushroom filling
500g/1lb 2oz large, flat chestnut or portabella mushrooms
500g/1lb 2oz large, flat horse or field mushrooms
60g/2oz dried mixed wild mushrooms or your favourite kind
4 tablespoons cold pressed extra virgin olive oil
1 tablespoon fresh thyme leaves
1 large garlic clove, crushed
Salt and freshly ground black pepper (don't use salt on detox)
Sprinkling of freshly grated nutmeg

**Lasagne**

150g (6 sheets) wheat-free, 100% corn lasagne

500g (2 cups) ricotta cheese

250g (2 cups) reduced-fat grated mozzarella cheese

Sprinkling of cayenne pepper

An ovenproof baking and serving dish about 33cm (13in) long and 20cm (8in) wide.

Preheat the oven to 180°C/350°F/Gas Mark 4.

- Make the tomato sauce first – you can make it the day before or freeze it in advance.
- Gently cook the onions over a low heat in the oil in a non-stick pan but do not brown them. Chop up the prepared tomatoes and once the onions are soft, stir the tomatoes into the onions along with all the remaining sauce ingredients. Simmer the sauce for 40 minutes, vigorously stirring with a wooden spoon from time to time until it is a soft pulp. Adjust the seasoning and then leave the sauce to cool.
- Make the mushroom filling. Peel and trim the various cultivated fresh mushrooms, quarter them and slice them thinly. Sauté them with the dried wild mushrooms in a big non-stick pan in the oil, over a medium heat, until they have softened, which will be about 10 minutes. Stir in the thyme and garlic and toss the mushrooms to ensure that they get evenly coated with oil and cooked through. Season the mushrooms with salt, pepper and grated nutmeg and leave to cool. They may also be prepared a day in advance, but not frozen.
- Spread a little less than half of the tomato sauce over the base of the baking dish. Cover the sauce with 3 strips of lasagne. You may have to break one piece and jiggle the pieces around to fit. Spoon the mushrooms all over the lasagne sheets, making sure that you take them right to the edges of the dish. Using a tablespoon, spoon the ricotta in blobs all over the mushrooms. Press down the remaining 3 sheets of lasagne over the cheese. Again, you may have to break one piece up. Cover with the remaining tomato sauce, sprinkle with the mozzarella and dust with cayenne pepper. Bake in the oven for 45 minutes or until it is a dark golden colour, bubbling and an inserted knife goes through the soft lasagne sheets.

## Coleslaw

Ready-made coleslaw is much maligned, but the home-made version is always delicious. Coleslaw is perfect for munching with a baked potato for winter lunches and delicious with new potatoes in their skins in summer.

*Serves 4 with baked potatoes or 6 as part of a picnic*          **GF WF V YF**

½ small firm white cabbage (400g/14oz), halved and very finely sliced
300g (11oz) organic carrots, coarsely grated
1 tablespoon freshly pressed bottled apple juice
5 heaped tablespoons virtually fat-free fromage frais
110g (¾ cup) shelled Brazil nuts, coarsely chopped
Salt and freshly ground black pepper (don't use salt on detox)
Dash Worcestershire sauce* and Tabasco* optional
30g (¼ cup) sesame seeds
15g (½oz) finely chopped parsley leaves

Put the sliced cabbage and grated carrots into a big salad bowl. In a small bowl mix the apple juice and fromage frais together and then combine with the cabbage.
• Mix in the nuts, salt, pepper, Worcestershire and Tabasco sauces (or their gluten-free equivalents). Sprinkle with the sesame seeds and parsley. Cover and chill the cole-slaw until needed but eat it on the day of making.

## Barbecued Vegetables with Dipping Sauce

The art of the successful barbecue is advance planning. Prepare and pre-cook everything you possibly can and keep chilled until needed. This way you will have time to enjoy the party too!

Do not be tempted to keep seafood, chicken or meat languishing around in the sunshine or near the heat of the fire, or there could be a number of upset tummies around.

Here are five easy recipes that all the family can enjoy. Each one will serve eight people. Decorate all the plates of cooked foods with sprigs of fresh rosemary or other herbs. You can easily add king prawns (jumbo shrimp) and chicken breasts to the barbecue. If so, then make up some more of the marinade for the spicy squash quarters and brush it over the prawns (shrimp) or chicken.

## Red Onions with Rosemary Dressing      GF WF DF V

3 large red onions, cut into 8 wedges
3 tablespoons cold pressed extra virgin olive oil plus a little extra for brushing
Sea salt and freshly ground black pepper
Cayenne pepper
2 tablespoons balsamic vinegar
3 teaspoons chopped fresh rosemary

8 bamboo skewers, soaked in warm water for 5 minutes

Thread the onion wedges on to the bamboo skewers. Brush both sides with the oil, season with salt, pepper and a light sprinkling of cayenne.

- Barbecue the onion kebabs for 30–35 minutes, turning from time to time and brushing with extra oil when necessary until tender and lightly charred.
- To make the dressing, mix together the balsamic vinegar, the 3 table-spoons of olive oil and the chopped rosemary. Drizzle over the cooked onions and serve.

## Sweet Potato Wedges                              GF WF DF V YF

You can speed up this recipe by parboiling the potatoes. It is a good idea to add a little lemon juice to the water to prevent discolouration. Refresh the semi-cooked potatoes under cold running water, leave them in cold water and keep covered until needed.

900g (2lb) medium-sized sweet potatoes, peeled and halved
Juice of ½ a small lemon (if parboiling)
2 large garlic cloves, crushed
4 tablespoons cold pressed extra virgin olive oil
3 teaspoons finely chopped sage
Sea salt and freshly ground black pepper
1 teaspoon ground paprika

8 bamboo skewers, soaked in warm water for 5 minutes

Parboil the potatoes in boiling water with the lemon juice for 10 minutes. Drain and refresh as suggested above.
- When you are ready to barbecue, slice the potatoes into thick wedges. Divide the wedges into 8 portions. Push them along each skewer, keeping them close together but not touching.
- Combine the crushed garlic and olive oil with the sage, seasoning and paprika, and brush it all over the potatoes. Cook over medium–hot coals for 20–30 minutes until tender and lightly browned.

## Spicy Squash Quarters                    GF WF DF V YF

Apply the same parboiling technique to these squash quarters as for the sweet potato wedges until they are just soft.

2 small butternut squash, quartered and seeded

**Marinade**
2 tablespoons cold pressed extra virgin olive oil
Sea salt and freshly ground black pepper
2 large garlic cloves, crushed
2 teaspoons ground cumin
2 teaspoons ground coriander
Sprinkling of cayenne pepper

Mix all the marinade ingredients together in a bowl and brush them over the parboiled but cooled squash quarters. Cook over medium–hot coals for 20–30 minutes until tender, turning occasionally.

## Charred Courgettes                    GF WF DF V YF

You could also use aubergines (eggplants) but I am so allergic to them that I cannot even touch them without coming out in a rash and definitely couldn't test the recipe for you, so I am afraid I will have to leave that one to you!

4 large courgettes (zucchini), halved lengthways
Cold pressed extra virgin olive oil
1 large garlic clove, crushed
2 teaspoons finely chopped fresh rosemary
Sea salt and freshly ground black pepper

Score a criss-cross pattern on the fleshy side of the courgettes (zucchini). Brush lightly with olive oil and sprinkle with the remaining ingredients.
• Cook the courgettes (zucchini) for 10 minutes, or until just tender, over medium–hot coals, turning occasionally until the courgettes (zucchini) are slightly charred at the edges.

## Dipping Sauce

GF WF DF V YF

2 tablespoons clear honey
1 tablespoon whole-grain mustard*
1 tablespoon lemon juice
4 tablespoons soy sauce* (yeast-free is available)
8 tablespoons tomato ketchup
Chilli sauce*, minced chilli in oil or chopped fresh chillies, according to taste
Salt and freshly ground black pepper (don't use salt on detox)

To make the dipping sauce, simply combine all the ingredients, then transfer to a serving bowl and serve with the barbecued dishes.

# Broad Bean and Spinach Frittata

What a marvellous way to get the family to eat spinach and broad (fava) beans, heavily disguised in this clever Spanish dish.

*Serves 4–6* **GF WF V (Omit the pecorino and butter for a dairy-free version) YF**

You need about 1kg (2¼lbs) of broad (fava) beans in their pods to give you 400g
   (14oz) of whole beans or 400g (14oz) of frozen and defrosted broad (fava) beans
250g (10oz) fresh spinach leaves, trimmed
6 free-range eggs
7g (¼oz) chopped flat-leaf parsley
60g (¾ cup) freshly grated pecorino cheese or other sheep's cheese, or
   dairy-free cheese
30g (2 tablespoons) dairy-free margarine or butter
Salt and freshly ground black pepper (don't use salt on detox)

25.5cm (10in) heavy-based, non-stick frying pan (skillet)

Cook the fresh or defrosted broad (fava) beans in boiling water until just tender, drain and refresh under cold running water. Pop the broad (fava) beans out of their skins and discard the skins.

- Meanwhile, blanch the spinach in a big pan of boiling water for about 2 minutes, drain and refresh it under cold running water. Gently squeeze the excess water out of the spinach and then lay it out on thick sheets of absorbent kitchen paper to soak up any remaining moisture.
- Beat the eggs lightly with a fork in a big bowl. Stir in the broad (fava) beans, spinach, parsley, ¾ of the cheese and season with salt and pepper.
- Melt the margarine or butter in the pan until foaming, pour in the egg mixture and turn the heat down as low as possible.
- When the eggs are on the verge of setting, preheat the grill (broiler). Sprinkle the remaining cheese over the frittata, slide the pan under the grill (broiler) and cook until golden. Transfer the frittata to a clean board, leave it to cool then cut into 4–6 wedges.

## Fresh Pea Quiche

Quiche is still such a good way of filling up family or friends for lunches, weekend picnics and holidays. You can make double the quantity or make mini versions for parties. Mini cup muffin trays, available from all good cook shops, are excellent for this.

*Serves 6*                                                    **GF WF V YF**

**Pastry**
250g (2¼ cups) wheat-free flour*
125g (4½oz) dairy-free margarine or butter, cut into 5 pieces
1 large free-range egg
Pinch of salt (don't use salt on detox)
A little cold water

**Filling**
1 tablespoon cold pressed extra virgin olive oil
1 onion, finely chopped
1 teaspoon herbes de Provence (mixed herbs can be used as an alternative)
400g (14oz) fresh green peas in their pods, shelled
1 tablespoon fresh tarragon leaves
4 large free-range eggs, beaten in a bowl
Salt and freshly ground black pepper (don't use salt on detox)
Freshly grated nutmeg
250g (1 cup) virtually fat-free fromage frais
Optional – 30g (¼ cup) freshly grated reduced-fat hard cheese and a sprinkling of
    cayenne pepper

A fluted loose-bottomed tart tin (pan) or quiche dish about 28cm (11in) wide and a
    circle of non-stick baking paper and some ceramic baking beans

Preheat the oven to 200°C/400°F/Gas Mark 6.

- Make the pastry by briefly blending all the ingredients, except the water, in a food processor until it resembles breadcrumbs. Add a little water and whizz briefly until the pastry comes together into a ball of dough. Remove the pastry, wrap it in clingfilm (plastic wrap) and freeze for 10 minutes.
- Heat the oil in a non-stick frying pan (skillet) and cook the onions over a medium heat until soft but not brown.
- Cook the peas in boiling water until tender, drain and refresh under cold running water. Stir the herbes de Provence into the onions and cook for a few more minutes.
- Roll out the pastry on a floured board into a large enough piece and gently lift it over the quiche dish. Line the dish with the pastry and even off the edges with a sharp knife. Prick the base with a fork in a few places, cover with a layer of non-stick paper, fill with a layer of ceramic baking beans and bake blind for 10 minutes. Remove the paper and beans, return to the oven and bake for another 5 minutes.
- Put the warm onions into a bowl with the peas, tarragon, beaten eggs, salt, pepper and grated nutmeg and mix thoroughly. Stir in the fromage frais until the mixture is evenly combined. Pour the mixture into the pastry case. Sprinkle with cheese and cayenne if you want to, and bake in the oven for 20 minutes until the pastry is golden brown and the filling is just firm.
- Serve warm or cold with a selection of salads.

## chapter 22

# Fish and Seafood

### Penne with Trout, Fresh Peas and Lemon

Peas have been found in Bronze Age settlements and were cultivated by the ancient Greeks and Romans. In medieval Britain, dried peas were the staple fare, but it was not until the 17th century that fresh peas were introduced from Italy and became fashionable. Now in the 21st century, they are canned and frozen! I hope this Italian-style recipe will revive the fashion for fresh peas.

*Serves 4*                                                            **GF WF DF YF**

2 fresh trout, about 525g (1lb 3oz) – get the fishmonger to gut (clean) them and
    remove the heads and tails
Salt and freshly ground black pepper (don't use salt on detox)
250g (10oz) pack wheat-free penne*
225g (2 scant cups) fresh peas
4 heaped tablespoons coarsely chopped fresh mint leaves
20g (¾oz) fresh flat-leaf parsley, coarsely chopped
5 tablespoons fat-free French dressing or cold pressed extra virgin olive oil for
    yeast-free diets
Finely grated rind and juice of 1 lemon
Minced chilli in oil, according to taste

Put a large pan of salted water on to boil. Meanwhile, wash the trout and season the skin with salt and pepper. You can cook the trout on a dish in the microwave until cooked through and opaque, but the time will depend on the size of each fish. Alternatively, steam, poach or grill (broil) the fish. I like to wrap them up loosely in foil with a generous sprinkling of water and bake them for about 20 minutes at 200°C/400°F/Gas Mark 6.

- Leave the trout to cool before removing the skin from both sides. Carefully lift the flesh off the bones and transfer to a plate. Pick out any remaining bones and then repeat with the underside.
- When the pan of water has come to the boil, add the pasta and cook according to the instructions on the pack, or until al dente. Drain and refresh under cold water. Use the same pan to boil enough water to cook the peas in. Cook the peas for 3 minutes, or until tender, then drain and refresh with cold water.
- Break the trout into fork-sized pieces, transfer to a pasta bowl and add the mint and parsley. Next, add the pasta and pour in the dressing, lemon rind and juice, season well and add the peas and chilli to taste. Toss the pasta salad carefully so that the trout doesn't break up and serve at room temperature, or keep chilled until needed.

## Smoked Trout and Guacamole Rolls

This is a great idea for picnics or a lunch box, and you can also fill the rolls with freshly poached or grilled (broiled) trout. If you would like to try this, then let the cooked trout cool, so that you can handle it. Remove the head, skin and tail and lift off the top fillets. Remove the spine and little bones and you will get to the bottom fillets. Fill the rolls with the trout fillets while still warm and serve with a mixed salad. One small trout will serve 2 people in this way. This recipe uses the famous wild Scottish trout, which is lovingly smoked and then sent all over the world.

*Serves 4*                                                                         **GF WF DF**

You can use this guacamole recipe at any time and the quantities can be doubled or halved.

### Guacamole

1 tomato, peeled
1 ripe avocado, preferably Fuerte
Juice of 1 small lime
2 spring onions (scallions), chopped
1 small garlic clove, chopped
15g (½oz) fresh coriander (cilantro), trimmed and chopped
1 fresh red medium–hot chilli, chopped (seeds removed if too hot)
Salt and freshly ground black pepper (don't use salt on detox)

### Filling and rolls

1 pack of 2 prepared wild Scottish smoked trout fillets, split into 4 pieces
4 warm wheat-free bread rolls*, sliced across but not all the way through

First make the guacamole. Cut the tomato into quarters, remove the pith and seeds and discard. Put the tomato flesh into a food processor or blender. Cut the avocado in half, and remove the stone. Scoop the flesh out of the shell and add it to the tomatoes. Add the lime, onions, garlic, coriander (cilantro) and chilli and process until almost smooth, and then scrape into a bowl and season to taste with salt and pepper.

• Transfer the guacamole into a bowl and cover with clingfilm (plastic wrap) or a tight-fitting lid and chill for 1 hour before serving.

• To assemble the recipe, just heap the guacamole filling into the roll and gently rest the smoked trout on the top. Close the roll and serve with a mixed salad and herbs.

## Thai Fish Cakes with Lime Dipping Sauce

My husband loves fish cakes, but for years I could not have them because they were always full of potatoes and butter, and covered with breadcrumbs – not ideal for those of us with food intolerances! My version is much healthier, and lighter too. You can make the fish cakes and the sauce in advance, but keep them covered and chilled until needed later in the day.

*Serves 4 as a main course, 8 as an appetizer*                    **GF WF DF**

### Fish cakes
450g(1lb) haddock or any other white fish, skinned and cut into chunks
1 garlic clove, crushed
1cm (½in piece) root ginger, coarsely grated
15g (½oz) fresh coriander (cilantro), coarsely chopped
Grated rind of 1 lime
½ red chilli, seeded and finely chopped
½ small red pepper (bell pepper), seeded and coarsely chopped
Salt and freshly ground black pepper (don't use salt on detox)
30g (¼ cup) sesame seeds
2 tablespoons wheat-free flour* lightly seasoned with a little salt and pepper (don't use salt on detox)
2 tablespoons of cold pressed extra virgin olive oil

### Dipping sauce
2 spring onions (scallions), heavily trimmed and finely chopped
1 tablespoon cold pressed sunflower oil
Juice of 1 lime
1 tablespoon saké (rice wine)
2 tablespoons soy sauce*
½ red chilli, seeded and finely chopped
2 teaspoons runny honey
2 teaspoons chopped fresh coriander (cilantro) leaves

For parties you can decorate with little chillies and sprigs of coriander (cilantro)

Briefly blend together the fish cake ingredients, except the seasoned flour and oil, in a food processor so that the mixture is minced but not a purée. Transfer it to a bowl and shape the fish cake mixture into 16 small, flattish rounds.

- To make the dipping sauce, combine all the ingredients together in a bowl and then transfer to a little serving dish until needed.

- Put the seasoned flour on a plate and then coat the fish cakes with it. Heat the oil in a non-stick frying pan (skillet) over high heat and fry the fish cakes until golden on each side. They will only take about 2 minutes on each side. Drain them on absorbent kitchen paper and then transfer to a warm serving dish and serve immediately with the dipping sauce.

- For a main course, serve these fish cakes accompanied by a bowl of crispy stir-fried vegetables.

## Artichoke Chowder

You can make a traditional chowder by adding 120g (½ cup) of chopped smoked bacon pieces, which you fry with the onions until golden, and 170g (1 cup) of prawns (shrimp) and 8 small scallops, which you add during the last 5 minutes of cooking. So that this recipe can be made for the vegetarian detox weeks, I have omitted these ingredients. I hope that you will make the more traditional version later.

*Serves 4*                                             **GF WF DF V YF**

Juice of ½ a lemon
500g (1lb 2oz) Jerusalem artichokes, peeled and coarsely chopped
1 small onion, finely chopped
1 large baking potato, peeled and chopped into small cubes
1 leek, severely trimmed and finely chopped
1 tablespoon cold pressed extra virgin olive oil
1 teaspoon fresh thyme leaves
1 bay leaf
1 litre (4 cups) of vegetable stock or boiling water with 1 heaped teaspoon
    vegetable bouillon powder* dissolved in it (yeast- and dairy-free is available)
A sprinkling of grated nutmeg
Salt and freshly ground black pepper (don't use salt on detox)
1 heaped tablespoon chopped fresh parsley leaves

Squeeze the lemon into a bowl of cold water and as you peel and chop the artichokes, submerge them in the water to prevent discolouration.

- Gently cook the onions, potatoes and leeks together in the oil in a pan over a low heat. Do not let them brown and ensure that they are softened before adding the thyme, bay leaf and artichokes. Cover with the stock and simmer for 40 minutes or until the artichokes are soft. Let the soup cool and then purée in a blender until smooth. Transfer the soup back to the pan and cook for a further 5 minutes over a medium heat stirring all the time.
- Season to taste with nutmeg and pepper, and remove from the heat. Serve sprinkled with the chopped parsley. The vegetarian chowder is very long-suffering and can be reheated again over several days, but sprinkle it with a little fresh parsley each time. (Always cool the soup, cover and chill in the refrigerator.)
- If you wish to make the traditional chowder, fry the bacon in the oil in the pan until crispy, then reduce the heat to low and add the onions, potatoes and leeks, so that they do not brown, merely taking on a golden tinge from the bacon oil. Add the herbs, artichokes and stock. Cook, cool and purée.
- Transfer the soup back to the pan, add the seafood and cook for 5 minutes over a medium heat, stirring constantly.
- Season to taste with nutmeg, salt and pepper, and serve immediately sprinkled with the chopped parsley.

# Crispy Scallops with Pak Choi

Scallops are expensive but you don't need many for this very light and summery main course. You can serve it with other oriental dishes and a bowl of fragrant steamed rice. Alternatively, serve it as an appetizer, providing 2 scallops per head.

*Serves 2 as a main course, 4 as an appetizer*                    **GF WF DF**

**Dipping sauce**

1½ tablespoons saké (rice wine)

1½ tablespoons soy sauce*

2 teaspoons runny honey

½ red chilli, seeded and finely sliced

1 spring onion (scallion), finely sliced

1 teaspoon finely grated root ginger

2 teaspoons finely chopped fresh coriander (cilantro) leaves

**Scallops**

15g (2 tablespoons) wheat-free flour*

Freshly ground black pepper

Pinch of cayenne pepper

1 tablespoon cold pressed extra virgin olive oil and a little extra for frying the scallops

4 baby pak choi, quartered

1 tablespoon Thai fish sauce*

Freshly ground black pepper

8 large scallops

First make the dipping sauce: mix the saké, soy sauce, honey, chilli, spring onion (scallion), and ginger in a small pan and cook for 1 minute over a medium heat, transfer to a small serving bowl, add the coriander (cilantro) and reserve until needed.

- Now prepare the scallops. Sift the flour, pepper and cayenne on to a plate. Heat 1 tablespoon of oil in a wok and stir-fry the pak choi for a few minutes so that it wilts slightly. Add the Thai fish sauce and black pepper and cook for another couple of minutes. Arrange the pak choi on a serving dish and keep hot.
- Dip the scallops in enough of the flour mixture to coat them. Preheat a non-stick frying pan (skillet) until it is very hot, add a drizzle of oil and then fry the scallops until golden. Do not over-cook the scallops, a couple of minutes should do. Drain them on absorbent kitchen paper.
- Arrange the scallops on top of the pak choi and serve immediately with the dipping sauce.

## Spiced Tuna on Noodles

For a stricter diet you can omit the noodles and replace them with plenty of coarsely grated raw carrots and courgettes (zucchini) – these should be stir-fried with the bean sprouts.

*Serves 4*                                                          **GF WF DF**

**Marinade**

4 spring onions (scallions), heavily trimmed and finely sliced

2 heaped teaspoons coarsely chopped fresh root ginger

1 garlic clove, crushed

2 tablespoons cold pressed extra virgin olive oil

3 tablespoons soy sauce*

2 tablespoons saké (rice wine)

2 tablespoons rice wine vinegar

1 tablespoon runny honey

½ red chilli, finely chopped (remove seeds if too hot)

**Tuna and noodles**

680g (1½lb) skinless tuna steak

125g (4½oz) straight fine rice noodles

2 tablespoons cold pressed extra virgin olive oil

250g (9oz) pack fresh bean sprouts

20g (¾oz) torn fresh coriander (cilantro) leaves, and an extra 7g (¼oz) serving

Chilli sauce* or minced chilli in oil, optional and according to taste

First make the marinade. Place all the ingredients together in a bowl, heat a wok over a high heat for a few seconds and then pour in the marinade. Cook for about a minute to release the flavours. Transfer the marinade to a dish in which you will be able to marinate the tuna strips and leave the mixture to cool.

- Cut the tuna into thin strips about 12mm (½in) wide, place them in the cold marinade, cover the dish and chill for 15 minutes. Now turn the strips of tuna over and marinate for another 15 minutes.
- Pour boiling water on to the noodles in a bowl, to soften them – about 3 minutes should do it.
- Drain them and then heat the oil in the wok over a medium heat and stir-fry the noodles with the bean sprouts, 20g (¾oz) coriander (cilantro) and chilli for a couple of minutes. Season to taste with pepper and salt if necessary.
- Transfer the noodle mixture to a warm serving dish and keep warm. Heat the wok again over a high heat and quickly fry the fish in the marinade, for about a minute on each side. Try not to break up the tuna.
- Carefully lay the tuna strips on top of the noodles and pour over the marinade. Sprinkle with extra coriander (cilantro) and serve immediately.

## Chargrilled Squid with Herb Dressing

Squid looks so off-putting, but in fact it is quick and easy to cook and not expensive. You can find it frozen all year round in the fishmonger's but do make sure he prepares it for you. You need whole cleaned tubes and the tentacles to be separate.

*Serves 4*                                                               **GF WF DF YF**

**Herb dressing**
45g (1½oz) flat-leaf parsley leaves
15g (½oz) fresh mint leaves
15g (½oz) fresh coriander (cilantro) leaves
1 teaspoon each ground cumin and coriander seeds
Finely grated rind and juice of 1 large lemon
4 tablespoons cold pressed extra virgin olive oil
2 small chillies, sliced
A pinch of salt (don't use salt on detox)

**Fish**
225g (3 cups) sliced runner beans (I like diamond-shaped lengths)
Freshly ground black pepper
12–16 small squid, prepared and washed (tentacles separated)
Drizzle of cold pressed extra virgin olive oil

To make the herb dressing, chop the herbs in the food processor but not too finely. Toast the cumin and the coriander seeds in a small, dry, non-stick pan over a medium high heat until they release a strong aroma, and then add to the herbs. Add the grated rind and juice of the lemon, oil, chillies and salt. Blend until finely chopped but not puréed.

- Cook the runner beans in boiling water for 3 minutes, then drain and rinse under cold water. Arrange the beans evenly over the serving dish, and sprinkle with freshly ground black pepper.
- Slit the squid open along one side and, using a sharp knife, mark a tiny criss-cross pattern on top. Cook the squid and the tentacles in a drizzle of oil on a preheated chargrill or in a preheated ridged pan for about a minute on each side.
- Place the squid in short rows diagonally along the beans. Spoon the herb dressing over the squid and serve immediately.
- This dish is delicious accompanied by simple salads, such as green leaves and herbs or tomato and cucumber.

## Chilled Halibut with Two Salsas

This is such a bright and cheerful summer dish. I much prefer chilled fish to warm – the texture is much firmer and I find the flavours are more concentrated. You can use cheaper seasonal white fish, or fish such as salmon, tuna and swordfish steaks. Serve this dish with a big green salad and some chilled French beans lightly sprinkled with lemon juice and olive oil.

*Serves 4*                                                                    **GF WF DF**

4 halibut steaks, around 900g (2lb) total weight including bone
Juice of ½ a lemon
Salt and freshly ground black pepper (don't use salt on detox)
4 bay leaves
4 wedges of lime to serve and a little fresh parsley to decorate

### Herb salsa

1 tablespoon capers* (not in malt vinegar), rinsed in cold water for 10 minutes
3 anchovy fillets, soaked in a saucer of cold water for 10 minutes
6 bottled baby cornichons* (cocktail gherkins) not in malt vinegar, drained
1 garlic clove, crushed
15g (½oz) mint leaves
15g (½oz) flat-leaf parsley leaves
15g (½oz) basil leaves
Juice of ½ a lemon
Approximately 5 tablespoons bottled fat-free French dressing and 2 tablespoons
   cold pressed extra virgin olive oil
1 teaspoon Dijon mustard*
Salt, if needed, and freshly ground black pepper (don't use salt on detox)

**Pepper salsa**

1 tablespoon cold pressed extra virgin olive oil

400g (14oz) can organic chopped tomatoes

1 medium–hot red chilli, finely chopped

15g (½oz) oregano leaves, coarsely chopped

1 garlic clove, sliced

1 teaspoon balsamic vinegar

2 small red peppers (bell peppers), seeded and coarsely chopped

Salt and freshly ground black pepper (don't use salt on detox)

Preheat the oven to 200°C/400°F/Gas Mark 6.

- Lay the fish on a baking tray, squeeze the lemon juice over, season lightly with salt and pepper, place a bay leaf on top of each steak and cover lightly with foil. Bake in the oven for about 15 minutes. To test if it is cooked, gently push a skewer into the thickest part of the flesh – if it is too firm then it is not ready yet. When it is cooked through, lightly cover the fish with the foil and leave it to cool.
- Make the herb salsa. Put the capers, anchovies, cornichons, garlic and herbs into a food processor and whizz until finely chopped. Transfer to a bowl and, by hand, stir in the lemon juice, dressing, olive oil and mustard and season to taste with salt and pepper. Transfer to a container to chill until needed but serve at room temperature.
- Make the pepper (bell pepper) salsa. Heat the olive oil in a saucepan, add the tomatoes, chilli, oregano, garlic, vinegar and peppers. Simmer for about 20 minutes or until the peppers (bell peppers) are cooked through. Cool the mixture before processing in a food processor, whizzing it to the consistency of a chunky purée. Season with salt and freshly ground pepper and transfer to a container to chill until needed.
- Once the fish has cooled, carefully remove it from its baking tray and put it on a dish in the refrigerator. To prepare the dish, gently peel off the fish skin, remove the bones and arrange the fillets in a line down the centre of a serving dish. Spoon one salsa down one side and the remaining salsa along the other side and decorate with the lime wedges and parsley. Keep chilled until needed.

## Roast Cod with Pineapple Salsa

Fish such as cod often crumbles and breaks up before it is cooked through. A good tip is to season it with a little salt two hours before you cook it, so that the protein in the fish will firm up and it won't fall apart. The unusual combination of cod and pineapple comes from the Caribbean-style idea of mixing fruit with fish. This has a refreshing sweet-and-sour effect.

*Serves 6*                                                        **GF WF DF**

### Salsa
1 small pineapple, peeled and the eyes dug out, quartered, core removed and flesh chopped into small pieces
1 tablespoon cold pressed extra virgin olive oil
1 tablespoon runny honey
400g (14oz) can chopped tomatoes
4 spring onions (scallions), heavily trimmed and very finely sliced
½ red chilli (any strength), seeded and very finely sliced
Finely grated rind and juice of 1 lime
2 tablespoons chopped fresh coriander (cilantro) leaves
Salt and freshly ground black pepper (don't use salt on detox)
Light sprinkling of cayenne pepper

### Fish
6 thick cod steaks or other white fish, must be thick enough to roast, about 900g (2lbs)
Juice of 1 lime
Salt and freshly ground black pepper (don't use salt on detox)
Sprinkling of cayenne pepper
Lime quarters and fresh coriander (cilantro) to decorate, optional

Preheat the oven to 200°C/400°F/Gas Mark 6.

- Make the salsa. Fry the pineapple in the oil in a non-stick frying pan (skillet) over a medium heat for about 3 minutes. Pour the honey over the pineapple and keep frying until the pineapple has lovely browned caramelized bits. Shaking the pan and stirring will prevent it burning.

- Remove from the heat, transfer to a bowl and stir in all the remaining salsa ingredients. If you are making this in advance, you can leave it to cool, cover it and chill it until needed but serve at room temperature.

- About 15 minutes before needed, put the cod steaks into a baking dish, sprinkle with lime juice, black pepper and cayenne pepper; there is no need to salt the fish if you did so earlier to firm it up.

- Roast the fish in the oven for 10 minutes or until opaque and just cooked through.

- Serve the fish on warm plates with a large dollop of salsa. Decorate with lime quarters and fresh coriander (cilantro).

## Swordfish Palermo

As the best swordfish is reputed to come from Sicily, I thought a local recipe full of traditional ingredients would be fun; this dish makes a nice change from the designer food so often eaten in trendy restaurants.

*Serves 4*                                                   **GF WF DF**

2 swordfish steaks about 340g (12oz) each
1 tablespoon cold pressed extra virgin olive oil
1 large red onion, finely chopped
2 garlic cloves, crushed
4 anchovy fillets, drained and finely chopped
400g (14oz) can chopped tomatoes
1 tablespoon chopped fresh rosemary
1 tablespoon capers* in sherry vinegar, drained
Salt and freshly ground black pepper (don't use salt on detox)
7g (¼oz) fresh flat-leaf parsley, chopped

Wash the swordfish steaks and pat them dry with absorbent kitchen paper. Heat a non-stick frying pan (skillet) until very hot and then dry-fry the swordfish for a couple of minutes on each side. Remove them from the pan and keep warm. Reduce the heat to medium and then, in the same pan, heat the olive oil and stir in the onions. Cook until soft but not browned. Stir in the garlic, anchovies, tomatoes, rosemary and capers and cook for 20 minutes.

- Season to taste with salt and pepper and then return the swordfish steaks to the pan with the sauce and simmer until they are warmed through.
- Place on a serving dish and serve immediately, sprinkled with parsley. Divide the steaks into 4 pieces at the table.

## Oriental Smoked Salmon

This is the ultimate easy appetizer, which I use all the time. The better quality the salmon, the smoother the taste will be. Cheap, oily salmon on special offer tends to be just that, oily, and tasteless. This recipe is also delicious with wafer-thin slices of extremely fresh raw salmon – my version of sushi!

*Serves 4*                                                                    **WF DF**

8 slices of good-quality smoked salmon about 50g (2oz each)
⅓ of a 90g (3oz) pack pickled ginger* (pink and sliced)

**Dressing**
1 heaped teaspoon Dijon mustard*
Salt and freshly ground black pepper (don't use salt on detox)
½ red chilli (any strength), seeded and finely chopped
2 teaspoons runny honey
2 tablespoons pickled ginger vinegar*
7g (¼oz) very finely sliced fresh coriander (cilantro) leaves
2 tablespoons cold pressed sunflower oil

Arrange the smoked salmon on a serving plate and carefully lay the pickled ginger slices over it.
• To make the dressing, mix all the ingredients together in the given order in a bowl. Sprinkle the dressing all over the salmon and ginger.
• Serve immediately or cover and chill until needed.

## Three Star Tostaditas

Quick and easy with no cooking, these nibbles are ideal as an appetizer for a barbecue while everything else is charring nicely over the charcoal. The tostaditas are also brilliant for drinks parties in the summer. Please note that while packs of corn chips may be gluten-free, the coating may not be, so check the label carefully.

*Makes 50 (serves 10–16)*                    **GF WF DF (one vegetarian) YF**

**Tostaditas with guacamole and prawns**
200g (7oz) king prawns (jumbo shrimp)
Juice of 1 lime
Pinch of cayenne pepper
½ garlic clove, crushed
200g (7oz) pack pure corn Nachips* or similar fried corn wafers* or Nachos* (for all the toppings)

**Guacamole**
2 tomatoes, peeled, halved and seeded
2 ripe avocados, preferably Fuerte
Juice of 1 lime
1 spring onion (scallion), heavily trimmed then chopped
1 garlic clove, chopped
15g (½oz) fresh coriander (cilantro), chopped
1 fresh red medium–hot chilli, chopped (seeds removed for a milder taste)
Salt and freshly ground black pepper (if making the guacamole as part of the detox, don't use salt)

First marinate the prawns (shrimp). In a bowl mix together the lime juice, cayenne and garlic and marinate the prawns (shrimp) for at least 1 hour, keeping them chilled until needed.
• Now make the guacamole. Place the tomato halves in a food processor. Cut the avocados in half, and remove the stones. Scoop the flesh out of the shells and place it with the tomatoes. Add the lime juice, onion, garlic, coriander (cilantro) and chilli and process until almost smooth, then scrape into a bowl and season to taste with salt and pepper.

- Cover with clingfilm (plastic wrap), or a tight-fitting lid, and chill for 1 hour before serving. To assemble this dish, just place a dollop of guacamole on to each Nachip, probably about 20, top with a prawn (shrimp) and sprinkle with coriander (cilantro).

## Tostaditas with sweetcorn and pepper (bell pepper) (V)

2 red peppers (bell peppers), halved and seeded
A little cold pressed virgin olive oil
1 teaspoon chopped fresh rosemary
300g (10½oz) jar sweetcorn relish*
7g (¼oz) fresh parsley, chopped

Brush the peppers (bell peppers) with oil and sprinkle with rosemary. Grill (broil) them until black patches appear on the skin and then peel off the skin with a sharp knife. Cut the pepper (bell pepper) into attractive slithers. Spoon dollops of sweetcorn relish on to at least 16 Nachips, decorate with the peppers and sprinkle with a little chopped parsley.

## Tostaditas with crab and mango

150g (5oz) fresh crab meat
Good squeeze of lime juice
A little chilli sauce* or minced chilli in oil
Salt and freshly ground black pepper (don't use salt on detox)
1 spring onion (scallion), finely chopped
About ½ a ripe mango, peeled and cut into attractive slithers or chunks
15 fresh basil leaves for decoration

Mix the crab meat with the lime juice, chilli, seasoning and onion in a bowl. Spoon dollops of the mixture on to about 14 Nachips and decorate each one with a little mango and a basil leaf.

- Arrange the three types of Nachips together on a big dish or several smaller ones and keep chilled until served. Do not assemble more than a couple of hours in advance otherwise they may go soggy.

**chapter 23**

# Meat and Poultry

## Chicken Kiev in Parma Ham

This is a health-conscious version of an old favourite. You need to make the garlic butter at least 4 hours ahead of time or preferably the day before in order for it to be completely frozen.

*Serves 4*                                                              **GF WF DF YF**

**Garlic butter**
110g (½ cup) soft dairy-free margarine (or unsalted butter which is not dairy-free)
2 large garlic cloves, crushed
Salt and freshly ground black pepper (don't use salt on detox)
5 tablespoons finely chopped parsley leaves
2 tablespoons finely chopped basil leaves

**Chicken**
4 free-range organic chicken breasts, skin and fat removed
12 thin slices Parma ham
Olive oil for brushing
60g (2oz) pack prepared wild rocket (arugula), washed
150g (5½oz) pack sunblush tomatoes in oil, drained

Preheat the oven to 180°C/350°F/Gas Mark 4.

- Make the garlic margarine or butter by mashing all the ingredients together in a small bowl with a small wooden spoon or, alternatively, in a food processor for a few seconds. Shape the mixture with clean hands into 4 equal sausage shapes, then squash them down with your hands, so that they flatten slightly. Wrap each one in clingfilm (plastic wrap) and freeze until rock hard.
- Using a sharp knife, slice the chicken breast down the length first, but not all the way through, and then deep into the width of the breast, but again not all the way through. Insert the frozen garlic margarine or butter into the pocket. Seal up the flesh, carefully enclosing the filling and bind it all together by wrapping each breast up in 3 slices of Parma ham.
- Brush the ham with a little oil, place in an ovenproof dish and bake for 25 minutes in the centre of the oven.
- As soon as the chicken breasts are ready, arrange the rocket (arugula) between 4 plates and divide the sunblush tomatoes between them. Place a chicken breast on each salad, spoon over all the juices and serve immediately.

## Rack of Lamb with Courgettes, Broad Beans and Mint

Having spent 10 years living near the borders of Shropshire and Wales, I have been used to the delicious Welsh lamb that our farmers produce each spring. This recipe melts in the mouth but needs to be served pink to get the best results.

*Serves 6*                                                          **GF WF DF YF**

2 racks organic lamb (6–7 bones in each one), for a less expensive recipe use a
    1.5kg (3lb 5oz) leg of organic lamb
2 heaped teaspoons Dijon mustard*
1 heaped tablespoon fresh thyme leaves
125g (4½oz) pancetta cubes or bacon cubes
450g (1lb) courgettes (zucchini), cubes
2 tablespoons cold pressed extra virgin olive oil
400g (14oz) can artichoke hearts or bottoms, drained and quartered
200g (1 cup) baby broad (fava) beans, blanched for 1 minute in boiling water,
    drained and rinsed under cold running water
1 large garlic clove, crushed
Salt and freshly ground black pepper (don't use salt on detox)
300ml (1⅓ cups) chicken or lamb stock
7g (¼oz) mint leaves, chopped

Preheat the oven to 180°C/350°F/Gas Mark 4.
- Spread the mustard over the skin of the lamb. Sprinkle with thyme, salt, pepper, and place the racks of lamb, mustard side up in a roasting pan. Roast in the oven for about 35 minutes, or until it is as pink as you like it, but don't forget that it will continue to cook for a few minutes once it is out of the oven. Remove it from the pan and leave it to rest for about 10 minutes. (If you are cooking the leg of lamb this will take about 45 minutes.)
- While the lamb is cooking, fry the pancetta and courgettes (zucchini) in the oil in a non-stick frying pan (skillet) over a medium heat until dark brown at the edges. Add the artichokes, stir in the broad (fava) beans, garlic, and season to taste. Add the stock and simmer for 10 minutes. Mix in the mint leaves and add any juices from the lamb and keep the sauce warm.

- Carve the rack of lamb and arrange 2 cutlets on a bed of the vegetable mixture on each plate and serve immediately, accompanied by a big continental dressed salad.
- (Carve the leg of lamb, serve all the vegetable mixture on one large serving dish and arrange the slices of lamb along the length of it.)

## Duck Breasts with Marmalade and Mango

Orange and duck has been an unfailing combination for a very long time, used by the greatest and the most famous of chefs and cooks. This is my simplified and updated version, which is very quick and easy. Remove the skin before carving if you are following this diet.

*Serves 2*                                                                  **GF WF DF**

Sprinkling of ground allspice
2 duck breasts, washed then dried with absorbent kitchen paper
Salt and freshly ground black pepper (don't use salt on detox)
½ ripe, medium-sized mango, peeled and flesh chopped into small cubes
1 heaped tablespoon pale orange marmalade
   Juice of ½ a large orange
Juice of ½ a small lemon

Lightly sprinkle the allspice all over the duck breasts and then gently rub it in with clean fingers. Season with salt and pepper.
- Fry the duck, skin down, in a non-stick frying pan (skillet) over a high heat for 6 minutes. Watch that it does not burn and turn the heat down a fraction if necessary. It should be dark and crispy.
- Meanwhile, mix the mango, marmalade and orange juice together in a bowl with a little salt and plenty of black pepper.
- Drain the fat out of the pan and discard it. Turn the breasts over and pour in the mango mixture, reduce the heat to medium and cook for 5 minutes.
- Lift out the duck breasts and let them sit on a carving board for 1 minute. Meanwhile, stir the lemon juice into the sauce.
- Carve the breasts into a fan shape with a very sharp knife. Lift each carved breast onto a warm plate and spoon the hot sauce around the base and one side.
- Serve immediately with steamed green vegetables.

# Beef with Celeriac Mash, Tomato and Olive Compote

I made this dish for my husband's birthday this year and it was utterly gorgeous, not only was the meat organic but properly hung and full of flavour. We eat far less meat than we used to but when we do, we really go for it!

*Serves 6*

**GF WF DF**

**Meat and marinade**

1kg (2¼lbs) trimmed organic beef fillet steak, or sirloin steak
1 tablespoon finely chopped fresh rosemary leaves
2 garlic cloves, crushed
60ml (¼ cup) cold pressed extra virgin olive oil
Salt and freshly ground black pepper (don't use salt on detox)

**Tomato and olive compote**

1 red onion, finely chopped
2 tablespoons cold pressed extra virgin olive oil
8 large peeled plum tomatoes, with the tops removed, cut into quarters, seeds and pith removed
1 garlic clove, crushed
1 teaspoon fresh thyme leaves
125ml (½ cup) vegetable stock, or water
1 tablespoon balsamic vinegar
85g (¾ cup) pitted black olives*, rinsed under cold water and then halved
24 basil leaves, torn

**Celeriac mash**

1 celeriac, peeled and cut into cubes
Juice of ½ a lemon
30g (2 tablespoons) dairy-free margarine
Grated nutmeg
Cayenne pepper
1 heaped teaspoon fresh thyme leaves
20g (¾oz) parsley, finely chopped for decoration

Preheat the oven to 200°C/400°F/Gas Mark 6.

- Make the marinade the night before cooking. Mix the rosemary, garlic, olive oil and seasoning in a little bowl. Lay the steak in a roasting pan and spread the marinade evenly all over it. Keep the steak covered and chilled in the refrigerator.

- Make the compote. Gently cook the onions in the oil in a non-stick frying pan (skillet) over medium heat for about 10 minutes, until softened but not brown. Add the tomatoes, garlic, thyme, vegetable stock, salt, pepper and balsamic vinegar and cook over a medium heat for a further 30 minutes, stirring from time to time. Add the olives and basil, cover the pan with a lid and leave until needed.

- Meanwhile, cook the celeriac in a saucepan of boiling water with the lemon juice until soft. Drain and mash until smooth. Beat in the margarine, salt, pepper, nutmeg, cayenne and thyme. Keep warm until needed.

- Roast the fillet steak in the marinade in the oven for about 15 minutes for blue, 20 minutes for very pink, or 25 minutes for pink (add about 5 minutes more cooking if using sirloin). Remove the steak from the oven and let it sit for 5 minutes before carving, as it will continue to cook through at this stage.

- Place a couple of large spoonfuls of the mash on to the centre of each warm plate. Carve the fillet, allowing 2 thin slices for each person and arrange them across the mash. Spoon a dollop of compote beside it and sprinkle with some parsley.

- Serve immediately with a bowl of dressed green salad leaves, for example rocket (arugula), baby spinach and watercress.

## Chicken and Basil Curry

Green curry paste is available in all good supermarkets or oriental stores and gives a lovely mellow flavour and silky texture. You can make a delicious vegetarian version using green beans, broad (fava) beans and courgettes (zucchini) instead of the chicken.

*Serves 6*                                                                 **GF WF DF**

1 tablespoon green curry paste*
2 tablespoons cold pressed extra virgin olive oil
2 large garlic cloves, crushed
2 stems lemon grass, finely sliced
2 lime leaves, shredded
2 x 400ml (14fl oz) cans half-fat coconut milk (Blue Dragon)
15g (½oz) fresh basil leaves, coarsely shredded
6 large organic chicken breasts, cut into diagonal pieces or 1 supermarket ready-
    cooked chicken, skin removed and carved into 6 pieces
2 green mild chillies, seeded and finely chopped
2 tablespoons Nam Pla* (fish sauce)
Finely grated rind and the juice of 1 lime
15g (½oz) fresh coriander (cilantro) leaves, chopped

Fry the curry paste in the oil in a big non-stick frying pan (skillet) over a medium heat for about 2 minutes, stirring occasionally. Add the garlic, lemon grass, lime leaves and half the coconut milk to the paste and cook for about 5 minutes. Stir in the basil, chicken, chilli and re-maining coconut milk. Simmer for about 20 minutes by which time the smaller raw pieces will be cooked, and the larger cooked chicken pieces heated through. Remove from the heat, stir in the Nam Pla (fish sauce) and the grated rind and juice of the lime.

• As this curry is almost soup-like, it is a good idea to serve it in warm bowls and then sprinkle with the chopped coriander (cilantro). If you are serving steamed fragrant Thai rice, then the rice will soak up the curry sauce and warm plates will be fine for serving.

## Chicken with Rosemary and Verjuice

We are used to the concentrated and deep flavour of balsamic vinegar, the lighter sherry vinegar and oriental rice vinegar, but now we are about to join the verjuice *(vert jus)* craze.

In French this literally means the 'green juice', which is extracted from unripe grapes. Ever since the Romans introduced vines to England, this juice has been used for cooking, and this only stopped when the vineyards went into decline. Once again, we have a thriving winemaking industry and our vineyards can produce this culinary delight to use in recipes from all over the world.

*Serves 4*                                                            **GF WF DF**

60g (generous ⅓ cup) raisins
200ml (¾ cup) verjuice (available from Sainsbury's special selection)
2 teaspoons finely chopped rosemary
1 large garlic clove, crushed
Salt and freshly ground black pepper (don't use salt on detox)
4 organic chicken breasts, skin and fat removed
1 tablespoon cold pressed extra virgin olive oil
60g (generous ⅓ cup) pine nuts
1 tablespoon finely chopped parsley

Soak the raisins in the verjuice in a bowl overnight. The next day, stir in the rosemary, garlic, salt and pepper.

- Arrange the chicken breasts in a shallow dish that is just big enough to prevent the breasts from touching each other. Pour the verjuice mixture over the chicken and leave to marinate for the rest of the day. Keep covered and chilled in the refrigerator.
- In a non-stick frying pan (skillet), sauté the chicken breasts in the oil for 5 minutes on each side over a medium heat. Add the pine nuts, cook for a couple of minutes, then add the verjuice mixture.
- Simmer for about 10 minutes, or until the chicken breasts are completely cooked.
- Lift the chicken from the pan on to warm plates. Spoon the sauce over the chicken, sprinkle with parsley and serve immediately with a selection of vegetables.

## chapter 24

# Desserts and Cakes

### Dark Chocolate Tart

This tart is perfection for a chocoholic, for any party or an Easter feast. A hint of cinnamon enhances the deep, dark flavour. You can buy sugar-free dark chocolate for ultimate luxury from Rococo in the King's Road in London (see page 260 for details).

*Serves 8*                                                    **GF WF DF V**

**Pastry**
200g (1¾ cups) wheat-free flour*
125g (4½oz) dairy-free margarine, cut into small pieces
1 large free-range egg
Pinch of salt (don't use salt on detox)
A little cold water

**Filling**

3 large, free-range organic eggs

4 large, free-range organic egg yolks

60g (scant ⅓ cup) caster (superfine) sugar

200g (7oz) high quality bitter dark (bitter sweet) chocolate*, broken into pieces
(this kind of chocolate should not have gluten or dairy in it but please check
label)

150g (5oz) dairy-free margarine


25.5cm (10in) non-stick loose-bottomed tart tin (pan)

Baking beans to blind bake the pastry


Preheat the oven to 180°C/350°F/Gas Mark 4.

- Make the pastry by briefly blending the ingredients, except the water,
  in a food processor until it resembles breadcrumbs. Add a little water
  and whizz briefly until the pastry comes together into a ball of dough.
  Remove the pastry, wrap it in clingfilm (plastic wrap) and freeze for 10
  minutes.
- Roll out the pastry as thinly as possible on a floured board. Lift it over
  the tin (pan) and gently line with it. Put a circle of non-stick baking
  paper on to the pastry base, fill with ceramic baking beans and bake
  blind for about 10 minutes. Remove the paper and ceramic baking
  beans and bake for a further 10 minutes.
- Put the eggs, yolks and sugar into a big bowl and beat with an electric
  mixer on the highest speed for 3 minutes until the mixture is pale,
  thick and creamy.
- Melt the chocolate and margarine together either in a bowl in the
  microwave or in a bowl set over a pan of simmering water. Stir the
  chocolate until smooth and then scrape every bit of it into the egg
  mixture. Beat with a wooden spoon until blended and then pour into
  the pastry case.
- Bake in the oven for about 15 minutes, or until the filling is nearly
  set, and then leave it to cool, out of reach of any passing cats, dogs or
  children!
- Transfer to a serving plate and serve at room temperature.

## Rosewater and Cinnamon Mince Pies

Christmas is very special to me. I love the spirit of giving and sharing, the traditional carols, music, feasting and just being with all the family in front of a roaring log fire. The excitement of decorating the Christmas tree on Christmas Eve, and the expectant joy of the children waiting for Father Christmas makes the days spent preparing and cooking worthwhile. These mince pies freeze beautifully; defrost them and bake them until they are hot and ready to eat.

*Makes 30 mini or 24 standard pies*                    **GF WF DF V**

**Pastry**
250g (2¼ cups) wheat-free flour*
125g (4½oz) dairy-free margarine, cut into 12 small pieces
Pinch of salt (don't use salt on detox)
1 large free-range egg
A little rosewater (available from superstores or pharmacies)

**Filling**
250g (1 cup) luxury mincemeat for the mini mince pies or 426g (1½ cups) for the
   standard size (vegetarian brands are available at health food stores)
¼ teaspoon ground cinnamon

About ½ tablespoon caster (superfine) sugar mixed with ½ teaspoon ground
   cinnamon for sprinkling
3 x 12-cup non-stick mini muffin tins (pans) or 2 x 12-cup standard muffin or
   mince pie non-stick baking tins (pans)
A fluted pastry circle cutter approximately 5cm (2in) for the pastry bases and a
   smaller cutter for the tops in a star shape for the mini pies, and 8cm (3in) cutter
   for the bases and 5cm (2in) cutter for the tops of the standard pies

Preheat the oven to 180°C/350°F/Gas Mark 4.

- Make the pastry in the food processor. Put all the pastry ingredients, except the rosewater, in the processor and whizz for a few seconds until the mixture resembles breadcrumbs. Cautiously add the rosewater, processing briefly until it comes together into a ball of dough.
- Remove the dough, wrap it in clingfilm (plastic wrap) and freeze for 10 minutes.
- Mix the sugar and the ½ teaspoon cinnamon together in a little bowl and leave until needed.
- Roll out the dough on a floured board into a medium–thick pastry and then cut into 24 circles. Line the cups of the baking tin (pan) with the pastry circles and prick the bases with a fork. Gather the remaining pastry, roll it out again with a little more flour, and cut out 24 smaller circles for the lids.
- In a small bowl, mix the mincemeat with the cinnamon, spoon about a teaspoonful into each pastry case and gently press it down as you cover the mixture with the pastry lid.
- Sprinkle all the mince pies with the cinnamon and sugar mixture and bake in the centre of the oven for about 15 minutes or until the pastry is golden and the mincemeat bubbling.
- Leave them to cool in the tins (pans) and then lift the mince pies out using a blunt knife. Leave them to cool further on wire racks. Warm the mince pies through before serving, or alternatively, freeze in an airtight container until needed.

## Lemon Muffins

I love zingy lemon recipes, which this one certainly is! It reminds me of the huge lemons that were growing in Portugal when my husband and I ventured into the unknown, and ended up driving around rather more of the Douro than anticipated. As everyone seemed to be involved with either harvesting vines or tasting wines, trying to detect a gastronomic pousada with an empty room each night involved hours of driving and map reading – all rather exhausting!

These muffins are great for picnics (top some of them with lemon icing for children) and the leftovers are still delicious for breakfast with fresh fruit and yogurt or yofu, or for lunch with fresh fruit salad.

*Serves 8–16 (halve the amounts for smaller numbers)*                    **GF WF DF V**

### Muffins
2 tablespoons poppy seeds
2 tablespoons runny honey
2 tablespoons lemon juice, *plus*
Finely grated rind and juice of 1 lemon
110g (½ cup) dairy-free margarine
110g (½ cup) caster (superfine) sugar
2 large free-range eggs
170ml (scant cup) plain live soy yogurt (provamol makes yofu) or a low-fat live
    goat's or sheep's yogurt if you are not sensitive to these products
200g (1¾ cup) wheat-free flour*
2 teaspoons wheat-free baking powder*
1 teaspoon bicarbonate of soda (baking soda)

12-cup muffin tin (pan) and a 6-cup muffin tin (pan) lined with 18 paper cases

Preheat the oven to 180°C/350°F/Gas Mark 4.

- Mix the poppy seeds, honey and 2 tablespoons of lemon juice in a small pan; bring to the boil over a medium heat and cook for a couple of seconds. Cool and stir in the remaining lemon juice and grated rind.
- In a food processor, beat together the margarine and sugar until smooth and then briefly mix in the eggs, yogurt and the seed mixture. Very briefly whizz in the flour, baking powder and bicarbonate of soda (baking soda).
- Divide the mixture between the muffin cups and bake for about 20 minutes until golden and springy to the touch.

## Baked Apples with Spiced Cranberry Stuffing

For the detox plan, try not to add more honey or maple syrup. For the rest of the season, you can add a little more if you have a sweet tooth. The bigger the apple, the more stuffing you will be able to fit inside, and it will help you to feel full.

*Serves 2* **GF WF DF V**

2 large cooking apples, central core removed (pulled out without splitting the apple)
40g (⅔ cup) dried cranberries or 85g (3oz) fresh, frozen (partly defrosted) cranberries
1 heaped teaspoon freshly grated root ginger
Finely grated rind of ½ an orange
½ teaspoon mixed spice* (pie spice)
2 tablespoons runny honey or organic maple syrup

An apple corer

Preheat the oven to 180°C/350°F/Gas Mark 4.
- Place the cored apples, so that they do not touch, in a small ovenproof baking and serving dish. In a small bowl, mix the cranberries with the ginger, orange rind, mixed spice (pie spice) and honey or syrup. Pack it right down into the cavity of each apple so that it touches the base of the dish. It is easier to start spooning the mixture using a teaspoon and finish pushing it down using clean fingertips. Let the remaining fresh cranberries tumble over the tops of the apples.
- Spoon 1 tablespoon of cold water into the dish, but not over the apples, and bake for about 25–30 minutes or until the apples are puffy and cooked through, but not to the point of collapse or bursting. Leave them to cool slightly in the dish, then transfer to warm plates with any juices, and serve.

## Passion Cakes with Passion Sauce

A romantic at heart, I need no excuse to create a special feast for St Valentine's Day or even just a quiet, cosy, candlelit dinner together to make the person you care for feel extra special. Heart-shaped tins are available from all good cook shops, some of which do mail order as well.

*Serves 2–4*                                                              **GF WF DF V**

60g (⅔ cup) ground almonds
30g (¼ cup) wheat free flour*, sifted
2 large eggs, separated
75g (⅔ cup) caster (superfine) sugar
1 teaspoon bitter almond extract
Flesh and juice of 6 ripe passion fruit (the more wrinkled they are, the riper)
Sprinkling of sifted icing (confectioners') sugar
Juice of ½ a small lemon
4 tablespoons Archers Peach Schnapps
Little exotic flowers or tiny sprigs of mint, if available, for decoration

4 heart-shaped baking moulds about 9.5cm (3¾in) in length lined with non-stick baking paper

Preheat the oven to 180°C/350°F/Gas Mark 4.

- Mix the ground almonds with the flour in a bowl. In the food processor, beat the egg yolks and sugar with the almond extract until pale and thick. Scrape the egg mixture out of the food processor and stir it into the flour. Quickly slice open 2 of the passion fruits, scoop the filling out and pour into the flour mixture.
- Beat the egg whites into soft peaks and fold into the passion fruit mixture. Divide the mixture between the prepared heart moulds and bake for about 15 minutes or until golden and springy to touch.
- Leave them to cool slightly and then turn them onto wire racks.
- Just before serving, place one heart on each plate and dust with icing sugar. Halve each of the remaining passion fruit; scoop the flesh out and into a small bowl. Stir in some of the lemon juice and all the peach schnapps. Taste to see if any more lemon juice is needed. Spoon the passion sauce over the pointed tip of each heart and into a little pool. Decorate with a flower or a few tiny sprigs of fresh mint.

## Prune, Almond and Cognac Tart

This is my winter favourite. The luscious combination of prunes, almonds and cognac matches well with warming winter game dishes or Sunday roasts. Because the mixture works so well, I have never tried an alternative to the prunes but if you are not a great fan, then I suggest trying ready-to-eat figs, and preparing the tart in the same way.

*Serves 6–8*                                                                    **GF WF V**

### Pastry
200g (1¾ cups) wheat-free flour*
125g (4½oz) dairy-free margarine or butter, cut into 6 pieces
Pinch of salt (don't use salt on detox)
1 medium free-range egg
A little cold water

### Filling
4 heaped tablespoons half-fat crème fraîche
2 large free-range eggs
120g (¾ cup) caster (superfine) sugar
125g (generous 1¼ cups) ground almonds
4 tablespoons cognac
1 teaspoon bitter almond oil or essence
60g (4 tablespoons) butter or dairy-free margarine
30 ready-to-eat stoned (pitted) prunes – if they are unavailable, use normal prunes, put them in a bowl of boiling weak tea to cover and let them soak overnight

25.5cm (10in) round, loose-bottomed, non-stick, fluted tart tin (pan)

Preheat the oven to 180°C/350°F/Gas Mark 4.

- Make the pastry in the food processor. Put the ingredients, except the water, in it and whizz for a few seconds until the mixture resembles breadcrumbs. Cautiously add the water and process briefly until it comes together into a ball of dough.
- Remove the dough, wrap it in clingfilm (plastic wrap) and freeze for 10 minutes.
- Roll out the dough thinly on a floured board and line the baking tin (pan).
- Beat together the crème fraîche, eggs, sugar, almonds, half the cognac and the almond oil in the food processor for a few seconds. Melt the butter in a small bowl in the microwave or in a small saucepan over a medium heat. Briefly beat the butter into the mixture.
- Drain and discard the liquid from the prunes, arrange them over the pastry base and then pour over the almond mixture. Bake the tart for 30 minutes, remove from the oven and sprinkle with the remaining cognac. Allow the tin (pan) to cool so that you can carefully lift the tart out on to a serving dish.

## Pumpkin Pie

You can use fresh or canned pumpkin for this recipe, according to the amount of time and space you have available. If you have children, it is great entertainment for them to scoop out the flesh of the pumpkin and make funny masks for Halloween.

*Serves 6–8*                                                    **GF WF DF V**

### Pastry
200g (1¾ cups) wheat-free flour*
125g (4½oz) dairy-free margarine, cut into 8 pieces
Pinch of salt (don't use salt on detox)
1 medium free-range egg
A little cold water

### Filling
200ml (¾ cup) bottled, freshly pressed apple juice
1 tablespoon wheat-free cornflour* (cornstarch)
425g (scant 2 cups) canned or freshly cooked pumpkin flesh, mashed until smooth
2 large free-range eggs, beaten
3 heaped teaspoons peeled and coarsely grated root ginger
4 tablespoons organic maple syrup
1 teaspoon mixed spice* (pie spice)
1 teaspoon ground cinnamon
A pinch of ground cloves
A little freshly grated nutmeg


25.5cm (10in) fluted, loose-bottomed tart tin (pan)

Preheat the oven to 180°C/350°F/Gas Mark 4.

- First make the pastry. Put all the ingredients, except the water, into a food processor and whizz for a few seconds until the mixture resembles breadcrumbs. Cautiously add the water and process briefly until it comes together into a ball of dough.
- Remove the dough, wrap it in clingfilm (plastic wrap) and freeze for 10 minutes.
- Roll out the dough on a floured board into a medium–thick pastry and then lift it over the baking dish and line it. Press it gently down to fit the dish, cutting away any remnants hanging over the sides. Prick the base with a fork and leave to one side while you make the filling.
- Mix the apple juice and the cornflour (cornstarch) together in a small bowl. Put the pumpkin flesh into a larger bowl and then stir in the apple juice mixture. Mix in the eggs, ginger, maple syrup and all the spices. When the mixture is smooth, spoon it into the prepared pastry case. Level it off and bake the pie for about 35 minutes, or until the filling is set and firm, and the pastry is golden.
- Serve the pumpkin pie warm.

## Raspberry and Pecan Roulade

Nuts, raspberries and cream are such a divine combination. In this recipe the roulade is made rather more slimming by using fromage frais. Consequently, we can allow ourselves the occasional indulgence when entertaining friends or family.

*Serves 8*                                                    **GF WF V**

4 large eggs, separated
Finely grated rind of 1 orange
110g (½ cup) caster (superfine) sugar, plus extra for sprinkling
Juice of ½ an orange
110g (4oz) pack walnuts or pecan nuts, chopped very finely
500g (2 cups) strawberry flavour virtually fat-free fromage frais (Onken)
225g (½lb) fresh, ripe raspberries

Swiss roll/roulade tin (pan), about 28 x 38cm (11 x 15in), lined with non-stick
   baking paper

Preheat the oven to 170°C/325°F/Gas Mark 3.

- Put the egg yolks and the grated orange rind into a large bowl and whisk briefly with an electric whisk. Add 75g (⅓ cup) of sugar and beat at high speed until thick and light, about 3 minutes. Add the orange juice, whisk on the highest speed for another 2 minutes, and then fold in the nuts.

- In a separate bowl, whisk the egg whites until stiff, adding the remaining sugar until you have firm peaks. Fold the egg whites lightly into the nut mixture. Spread this quickly and evenly over the prepared tray.

- Place the roulade in the middle of the oven for 15 minutes, until golden brown all over and just springy when lightly pressed with your fingertips. While the roulade is cooking, spread another similar sized piece of non-stick baking paper on to the work surface and sprinkle it lightly with a little caster (superfine) sugar.

- Remove the roulade from the oven and turn it out on to the sugared paper. Carefully peel the paper away from the corners of the roulade and discard it.

- Cover the roulade with a clean tea towel and leave to cool.

- Spread the fromage frais over the cold sponge, sprinkle the raspberries over the roulade and roll up. The easiest way is to take both corners of the short edge of parchment and gently roll the first third over the second, peel away the paper and flip the roulade on to the serving dish.

- Cover and keep chilled until needed. I make this a day in advance and it is just as good.

## Peach Angel Ring with Strawberry Coulis

This is such a delicious summer combination, with distant memories of the peach melba that we used to love as children. You can also use nectarines, but apricots are a little too dry for them to be a success.

*Serves 8–12*                                                    **GF WF DF V**

### Cake
125g (1 cup) wheat-free flour*
185g (1 scant cup) caster (superfine) sugar
Pinch of salt (don't use salt on detox)
7 large free-range egg whites
2 teaspoons cream of tartar
1 tablespoon Archers Peach Schnapps

### Peach filling and strawberry coulis
4–6 ripe peaches, peeled, halved, stoned (pitted) and thickly sliced
850g (3½ pints) ripe strawberries, hulled and wiped clean (or frozen and defrosted)
2 tablespoons rosewater

A large, deep, non-stick ring baking tin (pan) or a large, deep, non-stick *Kugelhupf* mould

Preheat the oven to 180°C/350°F/Gas Mark 4.

- Make the cake first. Sift together the flour, 7 tablespoons of the sugar and the salt in a bowl and set aside. In another larger bowl, whisk the egg whites at medium speed for 2 minutes, or until they are thick and foamy. Add the cream of tartar and increase the speed to high. Slowly sprinkle the remaining sugar into the egg whites and beat them until they form soft peaks. Add the peach schnapps and fold in the sugar and sifted flour mixture. Pour the cake mixture into the tin (pan) and bake in the oven for about 40 minutes, or until an inserted skewer comes out clean. The cake should be golden and firm to touch. Leave the cake to cool in the tin (pan) for 20 minutes, after which time the cake should come away from the sides.

- Ease the cake out and turn it on to a large serving plate. Fill the centre of the cake with the prepared peaches so that it looks pretty.

- To make the coulis, put the strawberries and rosewater into the food processor and pulse to a purée. Press the coulis through a fine sieve and discard the pips. The sauce should be thick, but just runny enough to spoon over the cake so that it trickles down the sides. Spoon some of the coulis on to the fruit and cake.

- Serve the rest of the sauce separately.

## Blackberry and Apple Tartlets

A brisk autumn walk in the country can be full of hidden treasures such as wild blackberries growing rampantly in the hedgerows and old orchard apples, which have tumbled to the ground, ripe and ready to eat. Make sure both fruits are ripe and juicy and then the recipe will be even more delicious.

*Serves 8–16*

**GF WF DF V YF**

**Pastry**

200g (1¾ cups) wheat-free flour*
125g (4½oz) dairy-free margarine, cut into 5 pieces
1 large free-range egg
Pinch of salt (don't use salt on detox)
A little cold water

**Filling**

1kg (2½lbs) sweet eating apples
250g (1½ cups) ripe blackberries without any stalks
Finely grated rind and juice of 1 lemon
Pinch of ground cloves
Sprinkling of caster (superfine) sugar (don't use for yeast-free)

A lemon zester
12-cup tartlet tray lined with non-stick baking paper circles (this is not necessary if it is a non-stick tray)

Preheat the oven to 180°C/350°F/Gas Mark 4.

- Make the pastry by briefly blending the ingredients, except the water, in a food processor until it resembles breadcrumbs. Add a little water and whizz briefly until the pastry comes together into a ball of dough. Remove the pastry, wrap it in clingfilm (plastic wrap) and freeze for 10 minutes.

- Using a lemon zester, peel thin strips of rind off the lemon and keep for decorating the tarts later on.

- Peel, quarter and remove the cores from the apples and thinly slice them into a pan with the lemon juice and the ground cloves. Simmer over a low heat until soft, stirring occasionally – this takes about 20 minutes. Gently stir in the blackberries and remove from the heat.

- Roll out the pastry thinly enough on a floured board so that you can cut out about 16 circles with a suitable-sized fluted cutter. Line 12 of the cups with the pastry and prick the bases with a fork. Fill them with the blackberry and apple mixture, sprinkle with a little caster (superfine) sugar and bake in the oven for about 25 minutes or until the pastry is golden.

- Leave them to cool and then carefully lift them out of the tray and on to a serving dish or wire rack. Make the remaining tarts in the same way.

- Serve the tarts at room temperature, decorated with a pinch of the lemon peel. They are delicious on their own, but some guests may like a bowl of virtually fat-free fromage frais or soya vanilla ice cream to delve into.

## Blender Fruit Smoothie

Fruit smoothies provide the perfect cocktail of vitamins and energy to start the day. You can use any seasonal fruits and, if you experiment with your favourite fruits, you will invent some gorgeous blends. You will soon have special textures and flavours that you like for different moods. Here are my two favourite combinations for summer.

*Serves 1*                                                    **GF WF DF V YF**

### Option 1
1 sweet apple, peeled, quartered, cored and sliced
Juice of ½ a lime
150g (1 cup) fresh, ripe raspberries
1 ripe, peeled and stoned (pitted) peach, coarsely chopped

### Option 2
1 ripe, peeled and stoned (pitted) nectarine, coarsely chopped
Juice of ½ a small lemon
100g (1 cup) ripe, freshly chopped pineapple flesh
1 sweet and ripe pear, peeled, quartered and core removed

Process all the ingredients for your chosen option in a blender until smooth. Pour into a glass and drink immediately.

# Conducting an Elimination Trial

This is the procedure for determining whether you have an intolerance to a specific food. It can be useful to follow the elimination trial before doing the detox.

## Which foods to test

If you're not clear which foods may be associated with your symptoms, ask yourself which foods you

a) tend to eat every day
b) crave the most
c) would find difficult to give up.

It's often the case that the foods we are intolerant to are the foods we crave and eat regularly.

## Time period

The optimum time period for an elimination trial is two weeks. During this period you need to *completely* avoid the food that is being tested otherwise the results will not be conclusive. Throughout the two weeks, monitor any changes to your symptoms and overall well-being. You may want to keep a journal and record any changes in your digestive health, energy levels and any other symptoms you experience.

## How many foods to test

It's important to have a healthy, balanced diet during the trial, so it's a good idea to only test a maximum of two or three food groups at one time.

## Before testing

You need to stock up on alternatives before testing a suspect food, and you should also spend some time preparing meal plans (the recipes in this book should give you some good ideas). This is an extremely important step, otherwise you run the risk of going hungry and not having a balanced and nutritious diet.

Plan your meals to take account of your daily activities. For example, if your normal routine is to have a sandwich at lunch, you need to make alternative plans during a wheat elimination trial, and this may necessitate taking a prepared lunch into work with you.

## Healthy alternatives

You can test both gluten-containing foods and dairy-containing foods simultaneously during a two-week period. To do this in a healthy fashion, it's essential to stock up on plenty of healthy alternatives, and here are some of the options:

- Gluten-free grains, available in health food stores. Eating these, along with other complex carbohydrates such as brown rice and dried pulses (legumes), will ensure you get plenty of good-quality energy foods and important nutrients such as B vitamins.
- Alternative milk products, including goat's, sheep's, rice and soya milk; goat's or sheep's cheese and yogurt.
- Healthy vegetarian sources of protein such as eggs, tofu (bean curd) and soya yogurt, and mineral-rich foods such as nuts, seeds and green vegetables.

## What to expect

It can sometimes (though not always) be the case that when a problem food is removed there is an initial negative reaction. This usually occurs during the first three to five days and can consist of symptoms such as headaches, lack of energy, an inability to concentrate, digestive disruption or a flare-up of symptoms that you are personally prone to. It's a good idea to start the elimination trial when you know you have a few stress-free days to rest if you need to. It can take a full two weeks to assess whether a particular food is affecting your well-being, so try to keep to this time plan.

## Reintroducing suspect foods

After two weeks of avoiding a specific food you should have a pretty good idea of whether this has made any difference to your well-being. At this point you can undertake a reintroduction test. This consists of a smallish meal containing the pure form of a food you have been avoiding. For wheat, choose a pure wheat cereal or a plain pasta (this is preferable to choosing bread which contains other ingredients such as yeast that can also be reactive). For dairy, try a glass of milk or a small piece of cheese (not blue cheese because it contains yeast). Monitor any changes in your symptoms during the next two to three days and notice any changes in your energy levels, as well as specific symptoms. Experiencing a drop in energy shortly after reintroducing a suspect food often indicates that sensitivity is present. Also follow the pulse test procedure given in Chapter Seventeen.

## Testing more than one food

If you test more than one food during an elimination trial, you need to do the reintroduction phase separately for each food. Follow the steps outlined above for just one food and notice your reactions during the subsequent three days. Then test the next food and wait for a further three days before testing the final food. When retesting multiple foods, it's best to stick with the elimination diet throughout.

## What to do next

If you didn't react to a food when it was reintroduced, there's no reason why you shouldn't include this food in your diet again. If the elimination and reintroduction trial does suggest that a particular food is associated with certain health problems, it's best to avoid this food in the medium term. Follow the guidelines in Chapter Seventeen.

# Shopping List for Non-Food Items

• *Denotes recommended items*

Juice extractor •
Skin brush (natural bristle) •
Jug water filter •
Blender
Coffee grinder or food processor
Fruit and vegetable washing solution
Tongue scraper
Toothbrush
Bicarbonate of soda (baking soda) •
Rebounder (mini trampoline)
Skipping rope
Skin exfoliating cream
Journal

## appendix 3
# The Cleansing Substances

*The main programme*
Flaxseeds
Psyllium husks (powder or capsules)
Milk thistle
MSM (2 grams a day)
Multivitamin
Vitamin C (1,000 mg)
Multimineral

*Additional for the stomach*
Apple cider vinegar (organic)
Vegetarian digestive enzymes

*Additional for the intestines*
FOS
Probiotic supplement (a good-quality one)
Glutamine (powder or capsules)

*Additional for the liver*
Dandelion tea
Glutathione

*Additional for the other channels*
Cranberry extract (powder or capsules)
Dandelion tea

*Other optional cleansing substances*
Lecithin granules
Wheatgrass powder
Other green food powders (chlorella, spirulina, green kamut)

# Foods Allowed on the Programme

• *Denotes Week One only*

*Fruits (fresh)*
All fresh fruits are allowed on the programme. Here is a selection for you to try. Buy organic where possible.

Apples
Apricots
Avocados
Bananas •
Blackberries
Blueberries
Cherries
Cranberries
Figs
Grapes
Greengages
Gooseberries
Kiwi fruits
Lemons
Loganberries
Mangoes
Melons (all types)
Nectarines
Papayas (Pawpaws)
Passion fruits
Peaches
Pears
Pineapples
Plums
Raspberries
Strawberries
Watermelons

*Vegetables*
All fresh vegetables are allowed on the programme. Here is a selection for you to try. Try to buy organic where possible (this is especially important for those that will be juiced).

Asparagus
Aubergines (Eggplants)
Beetroots (Beets)
Broccoli
Brussels sprouts
Cabbages
Carrots
Cauliflower
Celeriac (Celery Root)
Celery
Chicory (Endive)
Cucumber
Fennel
Garlic
Ginger
Green beans
Leeks
Mushrooms
Onions
Parsnips
Peas
Potatoes

Radishes
Spinach (raw only)
Sprouting seeds (all types)
Swedes (Rutabagas)
Sweet potatoes
Tomatoes
Turnips
Watercress
Yams

*Grains and pulses (legumes)*
Brown rice
Brown rice flakes
Buckwheat
Buckwheat flakes
Chickpeas
Haricot (navy) beans
Hummus
Kidney beans
Lentils
Millet
Millet flakes
Quinoa
Quinoa flakes
Rice cakes

*Fish*
Cod
Haddock
Halibut
Herring
Mackerel
Plaice
Salmon
Sardines
Sea bass
Sole
Trout
Tuna

*Meat*
Chicken (fresh, organic) •

*Vegetarian Protein*
Eggs •
Goat's milk
Goat's yogurt
Goat's cheese
Nut milk
Rice milk
Sheep's milk
Sheep's yogurt
Sheep's cheese
Soya milk
Soya yogurt
Tofu (bean curd)

*Nuts*
Almonds
Brazil nuts
Cashews •
Chestnuts •
Hazelnuts •
Macadamia nuts •
Pine nuts •
Pistachios •
Pecans •
Walnuts •

*Seeds*
Flax (linseeds)
Pumpkin
Sesame
Sunflower

*Oils*
Choose only cold pressed, extra
   virgin oils
Olive
Sesame
Sunflower
Walnut

*Herbs and spices*
Use any herbs and spices you like
while you're on the detox.

# Common Foods that Contain Wheat

This list refers to standard supermarket products. Where the item speci-fies 'many' please refer to the ingredients label and check whether wheat has been used. Please check the labels of all processed foods as wheat is frequently added.

Bagels
Batter
Biscuits/cookies (all)
Bread (all)
Breadsticks
Breakfast cereals (many)
Bulgar wheat
Cakes and muffins (all)
Chapatti
Crispbreads (many)
Croissants
Crumble mix
Cake and muffin mix
Cauliflower cheese
Chocolate bars and candy
Cheese biscuits and twiglets
Couscous
Curry sauce and chilled/frozen curries
Custard powder or sauce
Doughnuts
Dumplings
Durum wheat
Danish pastries
Egg noodles

Fish cakes or fish fingers
Fish in batter or breadcrumbs
Fish pie
Frozen desserts
French bread and French toast
Gravy powder
Macaroni cheese and lasagne
Mayonnaise (some)
Meat pies and puddings
Mexican dishes (enchiladas/tortillas/nachos)
Naan bread
Onion bhajis (but wheat-free in most Indian restaurants)
Pancakes or crêpes
Pasta (all)
Pasta sauce (many)
Pastry
Pitta bread
Pizza crusts or bases
Pot noodles
Quiches
Sausages and sausage rolls
Seafood in breadcrumbs
Scotch eggs

Semolina
Soup (many)
Spring rolls
Sauce mix (many)
Steamed puddings
Scones and crumpets
Sliced processed ham, turkey and
    meats

Vegetables in batter (e.g. onion
    rings)
Vegetables in breadcrumbs (e.g.
    mushrooms)
Vegetarian frozen dishes (most)
Vegetarian prepared foods (many)
Waffles
Yorkshire puddings

# Some Processed Foods that Contain Dairy Products (cow's milk)

Biscuits
Cakes
Cookies
Chocolate
Crêpes
Custard
Ice cream
Mousse
Muffins
Pancakes
Pizza
Quiche
Sauces
Soups

# Guidelines for Yeast Sensitivity

People who are dealing with a yeast sensitivity need to avoid all foods containing yeast or refined sugar. Here is a selection of foods that contain these ingredients.

Alcohol
Biscuits
Bovril
Bread
Cakes
Candies
Cheese (especially blue cheese)
Chocolate
Cookies
Dried fruits
Fizzy drinks
Honey
Ice cream
Jam (jelly)

Malted foods
Marmite
Miso
Molasses
Mushrooms
Soy sauce
Stock cubes (incl. vegetable bouillon)
Sweets
Syrup
Tea
Tomato ketchup
Treacle
Vinegar

In addition, it is important to avoid foods that may have mould residues (such as nuts that have been sitting on the supermarket shelf for a while).

# Useful Information and Addresses

**Antoinette Savill** has a website with news, helpful hints and recipes for 'wheat watchers'. The site also includes reviews of her other books, a credit-card hotline for purchasing books from HarperCollins*Publishers* and gluten- or wheat-free products from Wellfoods Ltd.
Website: www.wheatwatchers.com

**Dawn Hamilton** and her team of qualified nutritionists are available for personal nutritional consultations. These can be conducted face-to-face, by telephone or via the Internet. Dawn is also available for public speaking engagements and training seminars in health and well-being. She can be contacted at:

**Dawn Hamilton and Associates**
Suite 14035
Muswell Hill Broadway
London N10 2WB
Telephone: 0208 883 2408
email: health@drdawn.co.uk
website: www.drdawn.co.uk

FINDING A NUTRITIONIST
A nutritionist can arrange tests for food intolerance, yeast sensitivity and intestinal permeability, and develop a nutritional and eating plan that is suitable for your needs. The following two organizations can help you locate a nutritionist in your area:

**Institute for Optimum Nutrition (ION)**
Blades Court
Deodar Road
London SW15 2NU
Telephone: 0208 877 9993
Send a SAE with a cheque for £2 to receive the directory of qualified nutritionists.

**British Association of Nutritional Therapists (BANT)**
27 Old Gloucester Street
London WC1N 3XX
Telephone: 0870 606 1284

Send an A4 self-addressed envelope with 72p of stamps for a directory of qualified nutritionists. A voluntary donation of £2 is suggested to cover costs.

ORGANIZATIONS
**Coeliac UK**
PO Box 220
High Wycombe
Buckinghamshire HP11 2HY
Telephone: 01494 437278
Website: www.coeliac.co.uk

**The Vegetarian Society**
Parkdale
Dunham Road
Altrincham
Cheshire WA14 4QG
Telephone: 01619 280793
Website: www.vegsoc.org

**Berrydales Publishers**
Berrydale House
5 Lawn Road
London NW3 2XS
Telephone: 0207 722 2866

(*The Inside Story* food and health magazine)

STOCKISTS *(United Kingdom)*
**Wellfoods Ltd**
(Nationwide delivery of gluten-free and wheat-free flour and related products)

Unit 6 Mapplewell Industrial Park
Mapplewell
Barnsley S75 6BS
South Yorkshire
Telephone: 01226 381712
Fax: 01226 381858
Website: www.bake-it.com
Email: wellfoods@bake-it.com

**Community Foods Ltd**
Enquiries for stockists of gluten-free and wheat-free pasta and biscuits
(cookies)

Micross
Brent Terrace
London NW2 1LT
Telephone: 0208 208 2966
Fax: 0208 208 2906

**Doves Farm Foods Ltd**
(Nationwide delivery of wheat-free and gluten-free flours and related
products)

Salisbury Road
Hungerford
Berkshire RG17 0RF
Telephone: 01488 684880
Fax: 01488 685235
Email: mail@dovesfarm.co.uk
Website: www.dovesfarm.co.uk

**Simply Organic Food Company Ltd**
(Everything organic – fruit, vegetables, fish, poultry, meat as well as groceries,
baby food, wines and wheat- or lactose-free products. All delivered to your
home or office throughout the UK. Open 24 hours a day, seven days a week.)

Olympic House
196 The Broadway
London SW19 1SN
Telephone: 0845 1000 444
Fax: 0845 1003 020
Website: www.simplyorganic.net
Email: orders@simplyorganic.net

**C. Lidgate**
(Nationwide delivery of free-range and organic meats, eggs and delicatessen)

110 Holland Park Avenue
London W11 4UA
Telephone: 0207 727 8243
Fax: 0207 229 7160

### Organics Direct Ltd

(Nationwide delivery of baby foods, wines, beers and all organic produce)

Olympic House
196 The Broadway
London SW19 1SN
Telephone: 0208 545 7676
Fax: 0207 622 4447
Email: info@organicsdirect.co.uk
Website: www.organicsdirect.com

### Real Foods Ltd

(Nationwide delivery of 4,500 lines, including teas and cheeses)

37 Broughton Street
Edinburgh EH1 3JU
Telephone: 0131 556 1772

### Dr Hauschka Salon

(Fantastic creams and treatments for itchy hay fever eyes and other allergy-linked skin problems. Natural and holistic facials, massages and nail care. Also pure skin, make-up and bath products.)

4 Cheval Place
London SW7 1ES
Telephone: 0207 589 1133
Fax: 0207 581 7056
Email: renate@dircon.co.uk
Website: www.drhauschkasalon.co.uk

### Rococo

(Suppliers of sugar-free and dairy-free chocolate)

321 Kings Road
London SW3 5EP
Telephone: 0207 352 5857

NUTRITIONAL SUPPLEMENTS
**Biocare Ltd**
180 Lifford Lane
Birmingham B30 3NU
Telephone: 0121 433 3727

Biocare offer an extensive range, including an excellent selection of intestinal support supplements such as probiotics, FOS, glutamine (*Permatrol*), and digestive enzymes (including *Digestaid* and *Polysyme Forte*). They also offer specific formulations that support liver detoxification, such as *Hep 194* and *HepaGuard Forte* (both of which contain milk thistle). Mail order is available, or phone to get details of your nearest stockist.

**Higher Nature**
Burwash Common
East Sussex TN19 7LX
Telephone: 01435 882880

Higher Nature specializes in producing *True Food Form* vitamin and mineral supplements that are significantly better absorbed than many other supplements. Higher Nature also offers a range of superb digestive system formulations, including probiotics, FOS (in powder form), glutamine (in powder form), vegetarian digestive enzymes (*Easigest*) and psyllium husks (*Colofibre*). Flaxseeds are also available. The *Omega Nutrition* essential fatty acids (in liquid or capsule form) are excellent. Higher Nature products are sold in most health food stores; they also offer a mail order service and will send you a free catalogue.

**Solgar Vitamins**
Tring
Herts HP23 5PT
Telephone: 01442 890355

Solgar offers an extensive range of products, including three excellent multivitamin supplements (*VM-75, VM 2000* and *Omnium*). The *Earth Source Greens & More* is a fantastic green food powder containing wheatgrass, alfalfa grass, chlorella and a great deal more. They also offer a good range of herbal supplements, including milk thistle. Phone for details of your nearest stockist.

HOME CARE PRODUCTS
**The Healthy House**
Cold Harbour
Ruscombe
Stroud
Gloucestershire GL6 6DA
Telephone: 01453 752216

This company specializes in allergy-free homecare products such as cleaning aids, air purifiers, water distillers and bedding.
Phone for a free catalogue.

OTHER TITLES BY THE SAME AUTHORS
**Antoinette Savill and Dawn Hamilton, Ph.D.**
Also published by Thorsons
*Lose Wheat, Lose Weight: The Healthy Way to Feel Well and Look Fantastic!*

**Antoinette Savill**
Also published by Thorsons
*The Sensitive Gourmet: Cooking without Wheat, Gluten or Dairy*

*More From The Sensitive Gourmet: Cakes, Cookies, Desserts and Bread Without Dairy, Wheat or Gluten*

*The Gluten, Wheat and Dairy Free Cookbook: Over 200 Allergy-Free Recipes, From 'The Sensitive Gourmet'*

# Index